ALSO BY GÉRARD GAVARRY

Hoppla! 1 2 3

Originally published in French as *Façon d'un roman* by P.O.L éditeur, 2003
Copyright © 2003 by P.O.L éditeur
Translation copyright © 2011 by Jane Kuntz
First edition, 2011

Library of Congress Cataloging-in-Publication Data

Gavarry, Gérard.
[Façon d'un roman. English]
Making a novel, or how, following the book of Judith, I devised a story of the suburbs,
and with the help of the coconut palm, cargo ship, and centaur, thrice wrote hoppla! /
Gérard Gavarry ; translated by Jane Kuntz. -- 1st ed.
p. cm.
"Originally published in French as Façon d'un roman by P.O.L øditeur, 2003."
ISBN 978-1-56478-576-3 (pbk. : alk. paper)
I. Kuntz, Jane. II. Title.
PQ2667.A97474F3413 2003
844'.914--dc22
2011012691

Partially funded by a grant from the Illinois Arts Council, a state agency, and by the
University of Illinois at Urbana-Champaign

Ouvrage publié avec le concours du Ministère français chargé de la culture –
Centre national du livre

This work has been published, in part, thanks to the French Ministry of Culture –
National Book Center

www.dalkeyarchive.com

Cover: design and composition by Danielle Dutton
Printed on permanent/durable acid-free paper and bound in the United States of America

MAKING A NOVEL

or

How, following the Book of Judith,
I devised a story of the suburbs,
and with the help of the coconut
palm, cargo ship, and centaur,
thrice wrote *Hoppla!*

by Gérard Gavarry
Translated by Jane Kuntz

Dalkey Archive Press
Champaign / Dublin / London

If we call freedom not only the capacity to escape power but also and especially the capacity to subjugate no one, then freedom can exist only outside language. Unfortunately, human language has no exterior: there is no exit. We can get out of it only at the price of the impossible: by mystical singularity, as described by Kierkegaard when he defines Abraham's sacrifice as an action unparalleled, void of speech, even interior speech, performed against the generality, the gregariousness, the morality of language: or again by the Nietzschean "yes to life," which is a kind of exultant shock administered to the servility of speech, to what Deleuze calls its reactive guise. But for us, who are neither knights of faith nor supermen, the only remaining alternative is, if I may say so, to cheat with speech, to cheat speech. This salutary trickery, this evasion, this grand imposture which allows us to understand speech outside the bounds of power, in the splendor of a permanent revolution of language, I for one call literature.

—Roland Barthes, "Inaugural Lecture, Collège de France," translated by Richard Howard

EXPLANATIONS

In my experience, writing a novel has always involved the preliminary step of organizing a workspace: a place that brings together bits of experience, memories, blocks of private feeling, gestures, tastes, voices, landscapes, distastes, all connected in one way or the other to my life. Yet, before any writing takes place, I need to invent, or bricoler—*for it does come down to* bricolage—*a machine meant to denature all these odds and ends, so that by relinquishing my own story I'm in a way reprocessing it, with my affective freight kept intact only to be reinvested in a fiction now turned resolutely outward.*

It is one of these workspaces[1] that we will be visiting in the pages that follow. We will be finding out which materials were brought to bear. We will also learn what kind of machinery was assembled, what motor kept it running, and how the cogs meshed. In short, what are the means, the interactions—if not ceremonies—whereby it does occasionally happen that a novel gets produced.

---

1 That of *Hoppla! 1 2 3*—henceforth *Hoppla!* or *HL*.

THE PRIMARY ELEMENTS OF THE *HOPPLA!* PROJECT

The primary elements of the *Hoppla!* project were so mismatched as to appear irreconcilable.

What, after all, did I feel compelled to write about?

On the one hand, about the suburbs. On the other, about coconut palms, cargo ships, and centaurs. But also, and perhaps most especially, I felt compelled to write about Judith, the disturbing biblical heroine of the book that bears her name.

How was all this to cohere?

The project didn't really take shape until this double idea was in place: the book would be organized as a triptych, and then include a certain reversal.

The triptych form, with its three "panels," addressed an ongoing concern of mine: the desire to associate the principle of variation with that of complementarity. I had a model in mind, supplied by a volume of the *Adventures of Tintin*. Perhaps you'll recall the three parchments from *The Secret of the Unicorn*, and how they need to be superimposed and backlit in order for their message to be read in its entirety, revealing the location of pirate Red Rackham's treasure. This device suited my purpose—in many ways similar to the way we read the four Christian Gospels—and relates to storytelling in the oral tradition and indeed to all myths, several versions of which are generally passed down through the ages or coexist in the same era, at once confirming, completing, and competing with one another.

As for the reversal, it goes like this: my novel wasn't going to talk explicitly about centaurs, cargo ships, or coconut palms, but rather, coconut palms, cargo ships, and centaurs were to be mobilized in writing the novel. Rather than subjects, they would serve as rhetorical tools, each of which would in turn assist me in telling the same story of the suburbs—or, more precisely, the same story of Judith, as transformed into a story of the suburbs.

Judith, Briefly, and Her Transformation

Holofernes, general of the mighty King Nebuchadnezzar, after having subjugated the greater part of Samaria, has laid siege to Bethulia. Soon out of water and provisions, the inhabitants of the small Jewish town are growing desperate. Just when they are on the verge of surrender, a young widow named Judith, beautiful and pious, readies herself for a heroic mission: dressed in her most elegant clothing, she leaves the town in the company of her faithful servant to go present herself as a defector to the enemy camp; then, having seduced Holofernes, she takes advantage of the general's wine-induced slumber and lops off his head. In the aftermath of which the Babylonian army in great disarray is hacked to pieces by the emboldened Hebrews.

This in essence is what is recounted in the Book of Judith.

Now, from this story, what am I to retain for my novel?

First of all, the dramatic thread that, from a situation of collective defeat, leads to a lone and liberating murder—or at least one we may assume was so.

And then, a few key scenes or sequences, which we can break down as follows:

- invasion of Samaria
- lamentation of besieged Bethulia
- Judith determined to act, donning her most sumptuous clothes
- Judith and her servant descending into the valley where the besieging army is camped
- Judith's encounter with Holofernes
- Judith's slaying of Holofernes

But I will also be changing a good many things.

The time and place, to begin with. Everything will take place in the present day, in the suburbs, between Bagneux and Ris-Orangis.

And then, the initial premise. There will still be an assault, but not in the strict sense of an invasion or siege—and the assailant, besides, will be less a physical entity than a mode of being, a gesture, a word, an utterance standing in for any manifestation of the Intolerable.

Finally, I will invert the genders of the two main characters and scramble the letters of various proper names. *Holofernes* will thus become Madame *Fenerolo*, manager of a supermarket, while the same anagrammatic process will turn *Judith* into *Ti-Jus D*(eux-Rivières).[2] Likewise, *Bethulia* will become *Beuilhet* and will be used as the name of a street on the edge of the housing project where my "Judith" will live. As for the valley where the Babylonian army is camped out, this will become *Vallon Apartments*, located in the neighborhood of the same name, separated from the housing project by a large, muddy stretch of empty lot bordering a heavily trafficked road.

When all this has played out, it will produce three accounts telling thrice the suburban tale and thrice the gradual unfolding of the same

---

2 It is for the initial *D* that the characters of Bessie, Célestin, and their son Ti-Jus will be named Deux-Rivières, rather than Trois-Rivières (which is an actual place in Guadeloupe). In addition, the first name *Ti-Jus*, just as it evokes a certain Creole flavor, or more generally, a certain "tropical feel," also could stand as a diminutive for for *P'tit Jules*, *P'tit Julien*, or *p'tit jus* ("little juice"—slang for "a cup of coffee"). [Pronounced "tee-joo," and roughly translated as "Lil' Juice," the inversion and intended play on the syllables of "Judith" as pronounced in French *verlan* (what would be called "back slang" in English) would not function in translation, hence its appearing unaltered in the English version of *Hoppla*. —Translator's Note.]

dire fate—the rape and murder of a female supermarket manager by the son of one of her employees—with the understanding that rape and murder, just like landscapes, young people, or housing-project slang, will all be cast in the successive molds of coconut palm, cargo ship, and centaur.

THE COCONUT PALM WAY

At the outset, the *Hoppla!* workspace marshaled various elements comprising the project's "stock material." These were the characteristics peculiar to the coconut palm, to its morphology and growth, to the fruit it produces and to the industry and crafts related to its development. This involved various particular locations and situations, with all the gestures and attitudes one would ordinarily associate with these. It further included botanical terminology, whose special role will be addressed below, in the section entitled *COCONUT PALM JARGON*.

Once complete, all this material is found, both same and different, throughout the suburban fiction, where it steers invention and feeds the writing.

For example.

Not all coconut-palm trunks are perfectly vertical. Once outside coconut groves, you will see them grow askew—curvy, so to speak—some almost trailing on the ground, others twisted, arched, and even oddly sinusoidal . . . Now, let's jump ahead to look at the opening of "The Coconut Palm," first of *Hoppla!*'s three parts, which features a huge electronic map of Île-de-France on which points of light reproduce traffic patterns. The actual vehicles on the actual road-grid show up as points of light on the giant map. Same movements, same slow-down, same gridlock here or there, depending on whether things are flowing, stalling, or jammed.

> In the course of these transmissions, tiny points of light moved about the gigantic map, blinking on and off in a rolling *trompe l'oeil* wherever traffic was flowing smoothly, but

elsewhere barely twinkling, or already clustered into large patches, growing at the same rate and in the same proportions as their counterparts on the real network of streets, they would enlarge, stretch, and, incidentally, retract before resuming their entropic dispersal across the map; so that eventually, having been halted by a succession of stop signs and tricolor traffic lights, the automobile population in motion reached its maximum density on the highways out of Paris into the suburbs, by which time the entire map of Île-de-France was aglow with glittering trails of luminescence: elegantly arched trajectories, some weirdly sinusoidal, other sections impeccably straight, these being the most numerous, a jumble looking like the ruins of some immense multi-columned piece of architecture. (*Hoppla!* 1.01, pp. 5–6)

We see here how the "trunk roads," as the British say, make shapes reflecting both traffic patterns and coconut-palm trunks; or, rather, how by outlining the trunks of the coconut palm, they conjure up images of gridlock and contribute to the creation of a desolate suburban atmosphere; and, likewise, how by shading the text with a sense of disillusionment or dismay, this depiction of suburban despond depicts a real landscape only to the extent that it also implies a virtual coconut-palm universe (or, for that matter, any other sort of conceit for which either of them might serve as a metaphor).

Or again.

A coconut grove extends over several kilometers, sometimes dozens of kilometers along a coastline. The trees planted in a zigzag pattern create an indefinitely geometric design, airy and incandescent. For the coconut palm is a very airy sort of tree, and a very solar one as well. Its branchless trunk, you see, instead of nurturing a dark undergrowth, is always surrounded by a bright and empty clearing. As for its fronds, shiny, almost varnished, they offer no real impendent to the tropical light, which is broken down, passing through them, into striped shadows, the sort cast by striated shutters or open-work partitions.

But a number of the sunny regions where coconut palms grow are also hurricane-prone. Though the trunk is supple enough to bend under strong winds and resist uprooting or snapping in even the most extreme conditions, the fronds, on the other hand, are relatively vulnerable. Winds have been known to tear them right off and carry them away in a single gust, and in the wake of a hurricane, an entire coconut grove can be transformed into a grim vista where nothing remains but headless stumps.

Already we've accumulated a number of ideas that found several applications in the text. Among them:

The brief portrait of Ti-Jus that begins chapter 1.05 depicts him as a "solar" figure. This is because the young man was conceived as a sort of angel (of the exterminating variety), but also as a coconut palm:

> Perhaps it was his halo of wooly hair, his aerial silhouette, and a certain solar luster emanating from his person that all made Ti-Jus so popular with the girls. Willingly, women or young girls would allow themselves to come into contact with his skin, pressing their dresses or jeans, their undergarments, their bare flesh to it fearlessly . . . (*HL*, p. 21)
> Apart from his Afro-angelic "halo," which crowns this lanky

adolescent like a bouquet of palm fronds topping a slender branch, the confident and sensual postures attributed here to Ti-Jus's girls come directly by way of an analogy between Ti-Jus's body and the trunk of a coconut palm (which is, in fact, smooth enough to be comfortable or even delightful to lean against).

In front of the SUMABA (the supermarket managed by Madame Fenerolo, where Ti-Jus's mother Bessie works as a cashier), the streetlights that surround the parking lot are "planted in staggered rows" (1.02, p. 9). And on the Paris-Corbeil rail line, two trains pass "in a cyclonic din" (1.04, p. 19). And again, below the window of Madame Fenerolo's apartment, a car is maneuvering, making a noise "that could in no way compare with the silky, heartrending rasp that such tires would have produced on sand" (1.10, p. 48).

These are some of the ways the coconut palm leaves its mark and permeates the scenes of *Hoppla*.

Once the suburban setting is posited in the first chapters of the book, along with the "coconut palm way," and once the "manager-being," the supermarket manager as embodiment of contempt, is not only made manifest, but made manifest as something intolerable (1.03), it suffices to leave these elements to play out their respective destinies, according to the modified biblical scenario that I referred to above. Now Ti-Jus can appear, accompanied by three other tall, well-built teenagers. They are on the Paris-Corbeil commuter train, and since two girls have just come into the same compartment, the boys start hitting on them, pressing ever closer, getting dangerously aroused . . . The equivalence between boys and palm trees runs parallel here to that of their mounting, shall we say "masculine" excitement, and the menacing winds of the cyclone.

[T]hese same four were now getting increasingly agitated, and each in his own way. One stamped, as if pawing the ground, marking time, a fleeting wave running up his body to the back of his neck with each tread, bending him first in one direction, then the other. His neighbor stuck out his chest, broadening his shoulders; while a third, to keep a lock of hair out of his face, repeated the same cervical twist, over and over again, accompanied each time by a fresh snort, his head thus tossed around at the end of the neck as though swept up by some powerful cyclone. (*HL* 1.05, p. 25)

In chapter 1.08, Île-de-France is being invaded, and the Mermoz Projects (Beuilhet Alley) besieged, by the pernicious power of the manager-being. I imagine that, if the last remnants of local resistance were to yield to this force, the entire region would be subdued, devastated—which is to say, mapped onto the *Hoppla!* system, reduced to the arid, frondless coconut-palm landscape in the wake of a hurricane:

Here and there, in the dismal landscape, long, rectangular housing blocks will resemble recumbent towers. And the highways raised upon concrete piers will give the impression that the ground has collapsed all around them, or that a cataclysm has laid waste to everything, flattened whatever was once standing, except perhaps the highway construction works, a drab panorama of pylons overlooking the automobile graveyards and trailer parks, while a water tower or a steeple silhouetted against the horizon will stand out as the solitary survivors peering over the precipice at the end of the world. (*HL*, p. 38)

At one point, during the Paris-Corbeil episode, Ti-Jus, walkman in pocket and headphones over both ears, seems completely absorbed in the music, as if unaware of what he's seeing.

> As a result, the young man's eyes were free to roam. They might have lingered on the windows, mused at the odd assortment of real and reflected objects displayed there, or remained nonchalantly at rest in the quivering, striated half-light of their lashes. (*HL* 1.05, p. 22)

Or in the final scene:

> In the bedroom, meanwhile, shadows cast by a lampshade imprint their streaks onto the bedspread . . . (*HL* 1.11, p. 51)

In both cases, the streaks or striations have their origins in those created by the coconut fronds when silhouetted against the sky, or else casting their chiaroscuro imprint onto the sandy ground.

These first examples have sought to highlight the manner in which, paradoxically, the "stock material," having become essentially invisible in the text that it determined, is still present therein, having left its traces everywhere—lexical, dramatic, or otherwise. This persistence fluctuates between two modes: sometimes the coconut palm intervenes quite explicitly in *Hoppla!*, making an impromptu and unlikely appearance in the novel's suburban context; at other times, it remains buried beneath the fiction, concealed in the story's unspoken substrata and within the very intimacy of its language.

EXPLICIT COCONUT PALM

Unlikely, perhaps, but recurrent nonetheless—as dictated by *Hoppla!* logic—the coconut palm as such appears from time to time in the midst of suburbia . . . or at least in the midst of *Hoppla!*'s particular suburban sprawl.

This occurs when, to best depict one of those moments when everything falls apart in life, whether for an individual or a community, I chose to evoke a metaphorical bend in the road, and then the sudden absence of the coconut palms that, until then, figuratively speaking, had featured in our landscape—and the feeling, upon observing this metamorphosis, that one is now in new territory, and that from now on, nothing will ever be the same (*HL*, 1.03, p. 13).

This also occurs when, on the contrary, the text evokes the opposite moment, the inverse path, the return journey, the silent observation as one moves downriver, gradually approaching the estuary—and the eagerness to discover, bristling, in "the dark, jagged crest of the tapering forest," the first coconut palms (*HL* 1.05, p. 27).

This is the case every time the narrator's WE, or to be precise, the WE that at intervals departs from the storyline to remind readers of the novel's obliquely focalized first-person narrative mode, reaffirms that the novel is speaking from what I might call a resolutely "coconut-palm position" (which will become a cargo-ship position in the part two, and a centaur position in part three).

Thus, the opening of chapter 1.06:

> It might also happen that the stretch of water is ocean, with belvedere instead of the Lyon Bridge as the edge of the coconut grove, whence we gaze out to sea. We then try to imagine other shores beyond the horizon; but however well versed we may be in the range and dispersion of earthly locales . . . (*HL*, p. 28)

Or the end of 1.09, when Ti-Jus is preening before going out to make his delivery, and, accompanied by the "hulk with the comb" (avatar of the "faithful servant" of the Book of Judith), he walks toward the Vallon Apartments:

> And the jeans, jacket, and sweater he's wearing will impose their gaudy pigments on the landscape: sapphire blue— most precious of precious stones; heartbreak red—color of spilt blood; and yellow, too—color of the clayey earth after the first post-drought rains have fallen, making it gleam beneath our sandals with a brilliance akin to that produced by the varnished fronds and coconuts hovering over our heads . . . year in, year out. (*HL*, p. 45)

Or again, the penultimate part of the "Coconut Palm" section (1.11, p. 54)

> Homeward bound at last, Ti-Jus and his friend plunge wordlessly into the suburban night, puny shadows despite their size, as stunted as we ourselves might appear in other climes, when we go walking along the shore, exiting stage left, under the gaze of the coconut palms.

I reiterate, nevertheless, that the motif-title, according to my designs, should be taken as less a theme than a tool, meant to fashion a novel whose universe will remain apparently foreign to it, even antithetical. This is why, more often than not, the coconut palm plays its role with great discretion, if not complete self-effacement.

SURREPTITIOUS COCONUT PALM

We have already seen Ti-Jus on the Paris-Corbeil commuter train, where his obsession with music causes a division between his conscious mind and what his eyes are seeing; his instincts taking over, in a way . . . What I hoped to achieve by positing this situation was to bring about a moment where the protagonist would be able to appraise the population of the train car, searchingly but also involuntarily, his eyes stopping at each female passenger, assessing her various, shall we say, "feminine" attributes.

To put such a scene into words, which coconut-palm model might provide inspiration?

I chose the scenario of some agronomist surveying a coconut grove, assessing its overall health, growth patterns, productivity . . .

> [His eyes] drew a continuous horizontal line across the faces, halting suddenly, zipping into reverse, stopping once again, and, after a blink or two of their lids, commencing a kind of expert appraisal. They gauged someone's height, estimated someone's size, assessed a particular area of their bodies, appraised its volume, circumference, degree of ripeness . . . (*HL* 1.05, p. 22)

Further on, in chapter 1.07, where Madame Fenerolo has gone up to the Deux-Rivières apartment for a fitting, Ti-Jus has just come out of the shower and purposely lingers in the living room.

He then starts pacing, slowly, looking at the floor all around him as though keeping an eye out for the furtive and repeated appearances of some little burrowing creatures. As he does so, he uses his foot—with the agility of a soccer player—to pick up a ball of yarn that's rolled onto the parquet-finished concrete. Pausing then, he leans back casually against the wallpaper, against a doorframe. He blinks. He turns his head. With the towel, he wipes the inside of an ear or pats his hair dry . . . (*HL*, p. 34)

In this example, the underlying model is the fiction of a Ti-Jus character lingering on a tropical beach. He's drying off after a swim in the sea. The "burrowing creatures" he's looking for are the crabs known in the region as "coconut crabs." The ball of yarn he picks up "with the agility of a soccer player" is a coconut. The door frame he leans up against is the trunk of a coconut palm.

In the next chapter, I sought to express the concept of Refusal, which becomes manifest when the Mermoz Projects are faced with the intrusive display of the manager-being, marking a turning point in my narrative (just as Judith's decision to go over to Holofernes's camp changes everything for Bethulia). But I then came across the article "Palmales" in the *Encyclopédie Universalis*, where I learned that the germination of the coconut, like the fruit of all palm trees, produces first a primary root that quickly dies away, to be replaced soon thereafter by numerous adventive roots (several thousand) that grow tremendously long (ten meters or more). I pursued this germination idea in connection with Refusal—with the human organism as its seedbed—just as I would endow Refusal with the capacity to grow vertically, then to deploy harmoniously into the air, as do the trunk and the palm fronds.

Between the epigastrium and the pelvic region, in among the meanderings of our entrails, there germinates Refusal. We don't feel its corpuscular presence at first: only a thermal shift, an icy cold welling up from a place deep within us—deep, but nonetheless as far from the self as possible—and which, spreading unobstructed into our bodies, assumes the form of a thousand filaments merging with the complex network of our nerves. This intermingling disrupts the entire organism, all the way to the epidermal level, where, reacting to a phenomenon normally restricted to the viscera, the skin pales here, flushes there, and everywhere starts to crawl. Finally, when it outgrows the belly—as do pain or rage in similar circumstances—Refusal is externalized. It consolidates. It grows denser. It tapers off and shoots into the air to deploy its powerful waves of energy into the upper reaches of the enclosing space. And in doing so, it designs this space anew, reestablishing the curves and verticality that allow us to comprehend gentleness and to stand upright, the vanishing point that allows us to come and go freely, and the shadows that afford us a leisurely contemplation of full sunlight, and by making use of the same surroundings that have always shaped our lives, it reinvents the landscape as one capable of allaying our fears. (*HL* 1.08, p. 36)

Finally, in chapter 1.11, for the denouement, I devised the modalities of coconut-palm rape. Once more, I opted for an analogy that involved, in addition to a particular word and its double meaning, the recollection of a certain technique . . .

The technique in question is one used in a number of tropical regions for climbing palm trees, including coconut palms. You need a vine, or any strap sturdy enough for the job of girding together, neither too tightly nor too loosely, the climber and climbed. The former places the soles of his feet on the latter, leaning back into the strap, then in alternating movements thrusts backward and heaves upward, while his arms quickly slip the strap up a notch. Sometimes, making do with nothing but bare hands and feet, the climber will ascend with no support strap at all. In doing so, he needs to make up for the extra energy required by this stunt with swiftness of execution, almost as if he were walking up the tree trunk, body doubled over, in one continuous motion. As one might suspect, such a feat requires not only perfect timing and technique, but also the agility of youth, or indeed, that of a child.

And as for the particular word, it is quite simply the verb *mount*. Recall that besides its primary meaning—"to rise, to ascend"—it can also mean, not unlike *lay*, *screw*, and a few other options, "to possess sexually." The fusion, or superposition of these two meanings when applied to the double object of woman (explicit) and coconut palm (implicit), lies at the heart of the denouement, particularly in the following excerpt:

>(*The scene takes place on Madame Fenerolo's bed,*
>   *in the striated shadow cast by the lampshade;*
>   *Ti-Jus makes his move*)
>[A]rms pulling, feet pushing, fingers that loosen their grip
>only to grab on higher up, fingers grown numb by the

tightness of their grasp, no longer able to feel whether they're clutching at a soft or rough surface, flat or convex, smooth or uneven . . . Ti-Jus employs unbridled force, alternatively bending and unbending his posture, as though wanting to move forward, or else lift himself along the body that his embrace has overpowered, while the steep arch of his back and the tensing of his muscles lend bulk to his silhouette. This additional density calls upon abdominals and adductors as much as biceps and pectorals; and yet, more than any other part of his body, of the surface of his skin, he is compressing the palms of his hands, which are overheating, blazing, especially after slipping slightly, or, when shifting their grasp, they then recover their hold with a violent slapping sound. (*HL* 1.11, p. 52)

The action is clearly brutal, but you'll notice that this brutality is not at all conveyed by the details of its description, nor the language employed therein.

A clarification is in order here.

My choice of approach is very distant from, even diametrically opposed to any kind of naturalism, while, at the same time, my style, which is open to all available varieties of lexicon and syntax, is in no way a response to any concern for decorum or *belle langue*. Rather, these choices were determined by my aversion to conventional rhetorical figures, as well as to so-called spontaneous writing (which inevitably resorts to convention, in any case), and further by my resolve to rescue my text from any hint of sloppiness, and to preserve some sense of dignity for my characters. This explains why I refused to lock Ti-Jus and his friends into any such generalization as "youth," or worse, "kids from the projects," or to pattern them after some distant imitation of reality, or what passes for reality. I felt that this kind of simplification and mimesis would most probably amount to a fallacy, and undoubtedly to indecency (the indecency of mimicking people and reducing them to clichés, whether these be tourist photos or received ideas). I preferred to make my equivocal protagonists into coconut-palm beings, convinced that by doing so I would feel closer to them, and by taking this less-traveled path, I would stand a better chance of approaching something like a suburb-truth.

COCONUT PALM JARGON

To a great extent, going far beyond the confines of dialogue alone, it is in the peculiar lingo spoken by Ti-Jus and his friends that the text of *Hoppla!* (part one) is the most visibly, if not most actively driven by the coconut palm.

This language is a jargon of sorts, or something resembling jargon. Understood only by insiders, it comprises various borrowings, distortions, and wordplay, all having some connection to the coconut palm.

Thus, without having to search very far beyond the encyclopedia entry "Palmales" mentioned above, I now had at my disposal a whole botanical vocabulary; words with rather strange resonances designating the coconut palm itself (*Cocos nucifera*) or its various components: its trunk, also called its *stem*, which is a *stipe*; its pinnate leaf and its *foliole* leaflets, arranged in two regular rows on either side of the spine, or *rachis*; the flowering part of the plant, as well as the sheathing of this inflorescence—*spadix* and *spathe*, which is a large horn-shaped *bract*—and then its indehiscent fruit (i.e., a fruit that doesn't open spontaneously once ripe), called a *drupe*, a pitted fruit whose *albumin* gradually solidifies, becoming the *copra*, or coconut flesh . . . Also at my disposal were the many ways that palm fronds are used: braided and woven to make mats, baskets, hats, fans, roofs, partitions, palisade fences, to name but a few . . . I even found a recipe for palm wine—cut a spathe at one end, collect the sap that will gradually seep out, let it ferment . . .

With this scholarly vocabulary in hand, and granting myself the option to access whatever other elements of my stock material, so to speak, I might find necessary, I laid down two principles:

1. A line of dialogue formulated in this jargon should NOT be translatable into common language.

2. On the other hand, the intention or mood put across by the dialogue must be intelligible: friendly, mocking, sarcastic, insulting, threatening, flattering, etc.

I then only needed to borrow a few processes from the universal language practice called slang, which, by subverting or ignoring the norm, or playfully moving beyond it, forges itself a particular identity within common usage, and whose mere existence, depending on where and how it asserts itself, or what biases for or against it are provoked, can have the effect of a precautionary defense mechanism or, indeed, an outright assault.

One of these processes is *détournement*, or a kind of derailment of meaning. "What's with this Nucifera!" exclaims the hulk with the comb. Ti-Jus and his buddies make their debut at the same moment we're first exposed to their jargon. The reader is forewarned:

> Without even having to think, the silent witnesses to

this vocalizing identify the language they are hearing as French. Nevertheless, certain formulations sound odd to their ears; they can't quite make out certain words, or when they can, these seem to make no sense—as in the word *Nucifera* that one of the youths utters in annoyance when he tries unsuccessfully to open a door while the train is moving.

> "What's with this Nucifera!"
>
> "Spadices, dude, spadices!" says another, mockingly, both emphasizing, and elongating the *a*. (*HL* 1.04, p. 18)

Followed by:

> A third has gone over to rattle the handle on the bathroom door. He begs emphatically: "It's an emergency!" Pleased with his little joke, with his three friends looking on, he alludes to the *coir* of a *drupe*—says *drupe coir*, in fact, in the same sentence where he's just slurred *I can see from here* into *Ikn see from here*.

Nucifera, we will recall, is the scientific name for the coconut palm—*Cocos nucifera*. The *spadice* is its flowering part. These terms, already foreign to common parlance, are doubly estranging through the process of *détournement*.

Sometimes, however, strangeness is produced not as a result of a word's rarity but of the very commonness of the term or expression being *détourné*. For instance, on the Paris-Corbeil commuter train, the two girls from Maisons-Alfort are being preyed upon by the four Ris-Orangis boys when one of the former is lifted off the ground by the hulk with the comb. Her outrage finds expression in easily recognizable words that are nevertheless untranslatable, and no less incongruous than the other coconut palm jargon.

[S]o that, with the exception of several *weave the leaves*, some hate-filled *in palisade formations*, some panic-stricken *make some for yourselfs*, some *mats*, some *fans*, some *sliding shutters*, all belched out by the girl in the blue sweater, the last car of the Paris-Corbeil resounded with something less like human voices than some primal wind—muted, cavernous, and rising without warning to a strident pitch, like some random eolian howl. (*HL* 1.05, p. 26)

Or during the final rape scene:

The manager refuses to comply, turns her head, her face in profile and silent for a few moments, before at last yielding to the insistence of the one who now wants to hear her say *copra*—she says "copra"—*tar and copra*—she says "tar and copra." He wants to hear *wet sand* and *dry sand*. He wants *palisade*. He wants *roof, detachable doors, detachable shutters*, and, more, wants *lobster trap, mat . . .* (*HL* 1.11, p. 52)

Another process involves the creation of new words. The common practice of boring three holes in a coconut in order to drink its juice straight from the fruit gave rise to the curse *three-hole suck-juice* and its condensed variant *trisuckjuice*. Likewise, a verb can be derived from a nominal form, the way old French used to get along and African French still does today, whence the verb *to machetty*, which does not exist in standard French.

The boy next to him goes him one better. From *machete* he makes the verb *machetty*; from *conflagration, conflagro*. He says that, back at Thingy, at Whatsit, at Whatcha-callit, if they keep making *conflagro* with the *copra*, one of these days, he's going to *machetty* their *aerial roots*. (*HL* 1.04, p. 20)

*

Still another is distortion: inversion of syllables or letters, as in back slang; yes, but not quite; aphaeresis, which is the shortening of a word by dropping its initial sound, or else apocope, the omission of a final syllable or sound—all traditional devices as active in today's language as they ever were in the past, to which I add that of segmentation. Sometimes, the segmentation of a single word. *Nucifera*, for example, breaks down into *Cifera* on the one hand, and *Nucif* on the other—". . . finally letting out a 'Nucif!,' a 'Cifera!,' or some other laudatory exclamation" (*HL* 1.08, p.40). Other times, segmentation of a phrase, as is the case for the string of epithets hurled by the girl on the Paris-Corbeil commuter train (above), which originate not from any fully reconstructible discourse, but at least from a lexical field that can be reassembled with some consistency: WEAVE THE LEAVES INTO A PALISADE; MAKE MATS OUT OF THEM; FANS, SHUTTERS . . .

Need I emphasize that *détournement*, creation, distortion, segmentation, all these primary processes tend to work together, reacting to one another along with the relatively normal syntax and lexicon utilized in the novel to produce what is not quite a slang, but has the effect of slang.

An example:

> (*On the Paris-Corbeil commuter train,*
> *the four boys' insistent attentions toward*
> *the girls are growing more and more persistent.*)

The first to turn and face the boys—the less frail of the twosome under threat from the four-pronged formation leaning ever closer—asked in an unwavering voice whether the guys hadn't already had enough of a gust on their fronds. "Because of the trade winds," she added, seeming to suggest that this was hardly the proper time, season, or latitude. And in conclusion:

> "So, listen up! . . . Back into your hole, *gusbirs!*" (*HL* 1.05, pp. 23–24)

Incongruous as it might seem, this is in fact a classically consistent metaphor pertaining to the characters' identification with coconut palms (who have received a "gust on their fronds" from the wildly cursing girl previously lifted up by the hulk with the comb—much as one might say the girls had been "getting in their face" or "breaking their balls"). Some take the form of ellipses followed by contextual clues ("seeming to suggest that . . ." etc.) that are admittedly no less elusive. There is also an invisible beach lingering in this scene, with coconut crabs momentarily emerging from the holes they've bored into the sand, with a double process of diversion/distortion in French: The Latin for coconut crab is *Birgus latro*, so *Birgus*, in back slang, becomes *gusbirs*.

Further on, in the same chapter.

> *(The girl in the blue sweater lifted off the ground is hopping mad. She screams.)*
> "I'm gonna be weaving your *coir!*"
> Screaming now, more high-pitched:
> "I've got your *stipe dugout!*"

And finally, as if in a daze, her voice husky, growing more hoarse: you *spathes*, you *saps* . . . she had them *oozing*, she made them *ferment*; and with that, she freaked the fuck out of them.

So: is the recipe for palm wine recognizable in the last line?

In any case, taken together, I expect the examples put forward in this chapter will have provided an accurate depiction of the coconut jargon concept. In any case, they illustrate the following characteristics, which I will highlight here:

1. The jargon comes in bits and pieces. There are few scenes, few sentences in *Hoppla!* that rely entirely on this slang—or else few complete sentences where this slang appears.

2. The jargon is nearly always accompanied by some commentary or description of the circumstances of the speech act—facial expressions, intonations, emphases, etc.

3. The jargon occasionally shows up outside reported speech or the thoughts of a particular character, as if the entire text had been submitted to its influence—a text which in addition contains certain affectations, scholarly or scientific terminology, archaisms, and technical vocabulary, all elements which, though not strictly in the coconut-palm realm, are nonetheless related to the jargon, and chosen like the coconut slang to disturb our speech habits and our standard modes of understanding, and, despite its playful tone, to map the text's physical violence onto the area of language and meaning.

The Cargo Ship Way

Whether on the high seas or in port, we experience sensations aboard a cargo ship very different from those felt on dry land, and likewise experience different states of mind. These sensations and psychic states, as well as the physical realities that both generate them and serve as their backdrop, all this makes up the stock material out of which the second section of *Hoppla!* was conceived, outlined, and written.

As was the case for the coconut palm in part one, cargo ships are almost never mentioned explicitly in the section named for them. And yet, even more than with the previous motif-title, the effects are so wide-ranging that hardly a page goes by here that does not owe its existence to the world of maritime freight transport. Where the coconut palm intervened selectively to invent a new form of speech, to evoke a gesture or guide a situation, the cargo ship, in addition to its other functions, shapes the very space of our suburb.

Here's how.

The Feel of the High Seas

When you think "cargo ship," besides the vessel and its freight, you also think open sea—that is, a perpetually vacant, rounded surface in double contact with the celestial void and the enormous oceanic mass out of sight. On moonless nights, or when daylight thickens into gray, everything merges into the same opacity: near and far, up and down, the four compass points. In clearer weather, the slow, powerful rise and fall of the swells make the sea appear to be breathing. The crests are rounded, foaming only slightly, sparkling here and there. Or if the sea is glassy and still, nothing in the world seems to be moving, nor is there any mark on the surface save the ship's wake, a creamy figure constantly reborn behind the stern, opening up, widening as it goes, fleeing bit by bit and fading before disappearing altogether into the distance.

These few considerations inspired the following approach to conjuring up the Paris suburbs at the opening of "The Cargo Ship."

It begins at night—night being implicitly identified with the ocean: the overwhelming presence of the liquid element, sea and mist intermingling, underpinning that of the enveloping, penetrating gloom of the Île-de-France world.

> Not a sound to be heard. Nothing stirring. The nocturnal fog soaks the suburban lamplight, so that everywhere the same stagnant icy gray medium reigns, where earth and sky mingle, engulfing structures, sleepers, and vegetation alike. (*HL* 2.01, p. 57)

Then with sunrise, "atmospheric space" and "terra firma" grow more distinct from one another, the latter's flatness associated implicitly with the flat surface of the ocean. In order to evoke the mounting activity of a typical working-day dawn, I contrast zones of noise and movement with zones of silence and stillness—the first planes taking off and landing, the hovering of helicopters, automobile traffic, commuters converging upon the train station, employees getting to work or the opposite, neighborhoods whose inhabitants have already left for work. Noise and sound mount, in contrast to the silence and stillness of the vacated bedroom community. There is a "swelling" on one hand, an "ebbing" on the other, as suggested by the rolling sea; and soon, the oceanic-suburban fabric seems to be on the verge of tearing in two, under the influence of these opposing forces . . .

> Yet nothing of the sort happens. At very most, the movements of a few emergency vehicles set off a rippling motion at certain intervals, climaxing in a burst of sirens and rotating lights. Then, as though driven by the force of two opposing gusts of air, the congestions dissolve, become increasingly concentrated on the outskirts of Paris, scattered around the provincial edges, while the night gradually gives way to an overcast day, as foretold in the previous evening's weather report, looking much the same now as it will throughout the rest of day, and until nightfall, unchanging. (*HL* 2.01, p. 58–59)

In this already double-layered context (ocean + suburb), the rest of the first "Cargo Ship" chapter stages an encounter between two thirty-five-ton tractor-trailers, patterned after the meeting of two ships at sea. Caught in the same traffic jam, the trucks intermittently find themselves side by side. The other vehicles, the undulations of their hoods and their glimmering roofs, stand in for the water, and the dialogue between the two truck drivers imitates that of two captains calling to each other from their respective decks. Surrounded by the limitless stretches of the high seas, voices are quickly dissipated; likewise, from one thirty-five-ton rig to the other, dialogue proves difficult—because of the open sky and rumbling motors, and also because the two truckers don't speak the same language. Then, when one gets ready to pull off the highway (he will turn up again at the SUMABA), the two rigs diverge, honking their horns in turn by way of farewell, these sounding not unlike a ship's siren, thus producing in the ever-expanding space between them an acoustical effect similar to that which occurs on the ocean's surface when two ships sail away from each other.

When the first truck has started lumbering into the exit lane, once its driver has engaged its front-wheel axle, gradually steering the length of his vehicle into the right-hand lane—once, finally, he's hauled out onto the sloping curve of the exit ramp—the ever-widening gap between the two giant rigs is revealed, appearing immaculate, fresh, as though it's been sheltered for ages from all light and air. The pristine gap spreads, unhurried. Little by little, it gains horizontality, bringing with it the sounds of morning, wafting low over the suburbs, with nothing to impede its steady progress except perhaps during the time it takes for a truck horn to sound thrice, doubled by its echo—followed then by a short honk, and *its* echo[3]—the blaring baritone adieus called out from afar by the two truckers. (*HL* 2.01, p. 61)

Yet, to cross paths with another vessel during long-haul shipping, especially in such proximity, is a relatively rare occurrence. Such an event will provide material for gangway and steerage conversation well into the future. Ordinarily the lone solid object in an otherwise wholly liquid and aerial milieu, the lone manufactured object among the elements of nature, and also the only one to exist on a human scale with regard to time and space, the cargo ship is entirely

---

3   In the tradition of the merchant marine, this second short sounding of the horn, a final and optional one, adds to the simple farewell a tribute that the younger of the two captains pays to his elder.

isolated, and this isolation accounts for much in the way one feels when out on the high seas. It bonds the ship with its crew and cargo. It increases the monotony of days spent without touching land or coming into contact with any inhabited place, in a world of silence where the only sounds heard—and these exceptions are of paramount importance—are the roar of the engines and the lapping of the sea against the ship's waterline.

With "lone solid object" in mind, cut to chapter 2.06, to the Deux-Rivières apartment, where Madame Fenerolo has come up for a final fitting (have I mentioned that in addition to working as a cashier at the SUMABA, Bessie also does sewing out of her home?), and where a certain atmosphere is evoked:

> [I]n the absence of human voices, the various rinse, fill, and flush noises coming from the kitchen, or from neighboring units in the building—as well as the air, impalpable, floating through the apartment between floor and ceiling—all assign new meaning to their respective liquid and gaseous states, thereby underscoring the close affinity, as solids, between the objects, plants, and living creatures gathered together at the Deux-Rivières apartment.

Or a few lines further on (outside now, where it is nighttime):

> In such conditions, a walker feels as though he is moving into a landscape without boundaries, toward which fragments of his person rush, pointlessly, alone in the world, while he watches in close-up as they precede his face, subliminal. He is elated, almost delirious—yet steeped in the oppressive sense of existing in a place where none of his fellows exist. (*HL*, p. 81–82)

As for "monotony of days," chapters 2.09 and 2.10 occur in

uninterrupted succession, as if by enjambment, stretching out a scene treated far more elliptically in the other two sections of the novel: Ti-Jus, with almost sacramental gravitas, bears the package containing the wraparound skirt and pantsuit meant for Madame Fenerolo. The hulk with the comb accompanies him. They cross a wide vacant area on an embankment that overlooks Avenue de Paris, below which is located the Vallon Apartments. Everything in this episode flows from the idea of cargo ships and the feel of the high seas:

- Already, back at the Deux-Rivières apartment, while the boys are getting ready to leave.

   The visible presence of the space outdoors—so vast, and starting so abruptly just beyond the plate glass—was constantly prompting heads to pivot toward the windows. Bessie, like Celestin, yielded to this tropism; and even Ti-Jus, when he gives the signal for departure, will address his "Let's go!" less to his friend than to the wide, glittering world for which they are about to depart. (*HL* 2.09, p. 90)

What they are seeing is indeed the suburban space viewed from three stories up, but also the ocean, starting "abruptly" beyond the dock.

- Likewise, the words that delineate the mournful atmosphere in the apartment after their departure come straight from the port, and from the moment following the farewells after castoff, when the ship's wake, then the gradual disappearance of even the wake's last traces, sharpen the pain of absence.

   It takes Bessie's voice announcing that she's going to make dinner, or informing him of what menu she has in mind, for the domestic space to recover its wholeness, for it to become a pliable medium once again, open to the steady course of sound and silence, and in which nothing—not even a slight turbulence, not even the discreet stippling of a seamstress's stitch—remains of what had briefly disturbed it. (*HL* 2.09, p. 92)

Seen from the boys' perspective, however, the noises, sensations, and feelings are those of a progressive distancing from land toward the high seas.

The crumpling and occasional cracking of their leather jackets penetrated by the northerly winter wind as it whistles around their ears, as well as the endless rumble of traffic on the Avenue de Paris, have gradually eliminated the sounds of the Mermoz Projects, which, after having first been the place they'd broken away from, then the place they'd left behind, has now joined the land of Elsewhere—a space where compass points dance in constant and capricious flux. (*HL* 2.09, p. 92)

Or further on.

The vacant strip and empty sky recede before the boys' advance, recede all the way to the guardrail that lines the Avenue de Paris. Visible above the rail, the car roofs scintillate in an unlikely shimmering of heat, giving off inscrutable signals that could just as well belong to the gray, pale yellow, and mauve mass of clouds above them as to the grayish beige ground below. Every so often, against a background of noise that distance deadens and disassociates from the visible, a puddle laps at one of their shoes, or the kraft paper quivers, giving a dry rustle in the wind. (*HL* 2.09, p. 93)

• And again, the cargo ship is a place where women are absent. Or rather, a place where women exist only to the extent that they inhabit memory, the pages of magazines, the TV screen, or the imagination. Likewise, the girls referenced by the hulk with the comb are a mirage—to be precise, a mirage of lithe and bewitching bird-women inspired in part by Homeric sirens, in part by seagulls.

He eyes the terrain on all sides, as if there were girls to be had in droves right there on the vacant strip, all obligingly complacent, the wind teasing their garments, their gazes feverishly indiscreet, light and lithe, airborne, needing nothing more to propel their approach, withdrawal, or return than the smallest undulation of a hip or quivering of a lock of hair. (*HL* 2.09, p. 94)

• And finally—though I could add multiple examples—the sense of duration in crossing this vacant lot is similar to that experienced during ocean voyages where the limits and markers of space and time are blurred, and humans, surrounded by the silence of the elements, cannot help but follow suit and refrain from speaking.

The monologue stops there, leaving the walkers' silence to rub grimly against the silence of the deserted strip. Time passes uneventfully, marked only by the repetition of footsteps that fall as though by routine, outside any prospect of arrival and beyond the memory of any departure. (*HL* 2.10, p. 96)

THE IDEA OF LAND

Woman as island

Though isolated or insular by virtue of its oceanic location, water on all sides, the cargo ship is not exactly an island. The pitching of the deck beneath one's feet and the shuddering of the engines reverberate throughout one's body, incessantly reactivating the idea that one is afloat and in flux, exiled not only from countries and people but from land itself, which becomes what the navigator longs for most: not there, not there yet, still not there . . . Or if land happens to appear on the horizon, an islet or cape lingering in view for a few minutes or hours or a strip of coastline edging past for several days, in the end it always returns to nothingness, causing one to wonder whether its appearance was not simply a projection.

Absent, and therefore object of reverie or reminiscence, of temptation, rejection, or frustration, such is any land from the cargo-ship viewpoint—as will be for Ti-Jus all women, physically and geographically.

He says to himself, "I'll get there, someday I'll get there." Such sensual expectations! Rock-solid ground underfoot; to walk upon, or run, or to take one's rest; the eye embraces many a place down below, many a place displaying its slopes and shadows, its crests, its sun-drenched valleys, exuding its earthly scents, the sound of its flora rustling intermittently, its brooks babbling. (*HL* 2.07, p. 86)

A bit earlier, arriving back home on foot from the commuter train station, Ti-Jus had caught sight of Madame Fenerolo at a distance.

Here's the pattern chosen to model the scene: this time, not a port of call where the seaman finds some earthly paradise, but an earlier stage with the same seaman watching an island draw nearer as more and more of its features come into focus.

> Had the manager remained stationary, the young man would have seen her grow larger bit by bit, finally taking shape. The standard feminine outline of the first instants would have gradually broken up into various zones—head, trunk, limbs—or into even and uneven zones—convex or concave—then neck, face, hair, gloved and ungloved hands, high heels, left and right ankles, as well as the parts of both legs located between pelisse and ankle. (*HL*, 2.06, p. 82)

Also from the same woman/island analogy comes Madame Fenerolo's seductive perfume, in which hints of a fictitious "wild island blackberry" blend with more realistic lemon and camphor overtones. And again, since she is associated with the element of earth, at the end of the section, when Ti-Jus and the hulk with the comb arrive at her apartment (2.11), she is wearing gardening gloves and is surrounded by the scent of humus-laden household potting soil, while the boys, like two sailors straight off the boat, permeated by marine odors, still bear the more feral smells of the vacant lot they've just traversed, with hints of "clay, cold rust, and exhaust fumes."

Departure, arrival, departure

Departure, arrival, departure . . . This is the rhythm of all nomads. But the cargo ship, more so than the gypsy wagon or the desert caravan, conveys the idea of a world beyond, the sense that the vessel itself, a mass so enormous that one is surprised it can remain afloat, is the stuff of those phantoms that appear on and off in the solid here and now of the living, though belonging more to the timelessness of the unseen faraway and of the dead.

It is always "the pilot"—term used to designate the specialized coastal navigator—whose local knowledge helps steer ships into and out of the harbor. The "pilot boat," his own craft, first takes him out to meet the newly arrived vessel. He climbs aboard on a rope ladder that the deckhands lower down to him, with other sailors holding it steady below as the pilot ascends vertically rung by rung along the hull. He is greeted with a cordiality bordering on deference, is served coffee or another non-alcoholic beverage. Finally, having assumed command of the wheelhouse, he begins transmitting his orders one by one to the helmsman, who repeats them out loud in the same order and scrupulously executes each command, the two seamen proceeding thus to maneuver the vessel until the double signal to drop anchor and stop engines is given.

It often happens that a ship has to drop anchor out in the harbor until a dock frees up, or until the quarantine imposed by local health authorities has expired (in the past, a forty-day period during which the ship was to fly a black-and-yellow checkered flag). Apart from these exceptions, the ship sails right into dock and moors, either parallel to, facing, or abutting the wharf.

All this cargo-ship data was gathered for the *Hoppla!* workspace so that I could find suburban applications for it.

Thus, when the thirty-five-ton sixteen-wheeler from chapter 2.01 arrives at the SUMABA, it will do so by slowly emerging from the surrounding predawn gloom and only gradually assume its full heft.

> The night watchman and the daytime security guards, the meat-counter staff in their civvies, and the slaughterhouse people in white overcoats all pause as well. Beneath the soles of their feet, as well as deep inside their leg bones, they are experiencing vibrations whose cause can't be perceived by eye or ear; and several seconds pass like this before they begin to hear an unidentifiable rumble, muted and continuous, and then several more seconds pass before they begin to make out the arrival and then gradual enlargement of a certain glow beaming through the screen of foggy half-light in front of them. Then, glow and rumble combined take shape, become radiator grill, become truck. And only then does the entire vehicle emerge, move forward, colossal and cautious, as though taking great pains, even feeling regret, needing now to return to the visible world after so protracted an isolation in the ghostly realms. (*HL*, 2.02, p. 63)

And again, when the same thirty-five-ton rig moves back off into the distance, a helicopter "alone in the whitish sameness of the sky" will fly toward it, come within reach, hover low for a while, nearly touching it, then will "regain its former altitude and speed" as it "curves around, and heads straight back to Bagneux." This is a scene patterned after that of a pilot boat heading out to pick up its pilot and then bringing him back to port as the cargo ship that he has just maneuvered out sails off to sea.

Or when Ti-Jus and his buddies appear at the end of a narrow street, suddenly blocking it with their four-pronged presence, they will be arranged like ships at dock.

> One of them was smoking. Ciggy clinging to one lip, he paid no heed to the rain—or else was defying it—his young, ascetic face turned up into the weather, into the vertical beams of the streetlamp. Behind him, the hulk with the comb rocked lazily from one foot to the other, while the third friend, left hand extended obliquely toward the ground, snapped his fingers to the rhythm of a lullaby. Ti-Jus, alone, his hair pearled with droplets, then turned his back to the street that the foursome's sudden appearance had left speechless. He stood at a slight distance from his friends, arms brought symmetrically forward, legs straight, feet spread: the pissing boy position. (*HL* 2.04, p. 72)

The boys' arms and legs mimic moorings. The lullaby tempo matches the imperceptible roll that continues to rock the ship, despite the multiple moorings. Ti-Jus abuts the wharf. The words "pissing boy" are there mainly to introduce a sexual connotation and a touch of wildness, but they also reinforce the falling rain and the droplets pearling his hair (done in dreadlocks, by the way) to help "liquefy" the scene overall.

And since my four suburban boys are secretly cargo ships at dock, or temporarily idling sailors leaning over the railings, when one of them flicks his cigarette butt, it falls much farther than the mere height of a man and ends its trajectory in seawater that has become rainwater on pavement, having nevertheless kept the murky, oily, and pungent memory of the waters at port.

> [T]he projectile landed in a freefall after completing a brief arc; the fall was endless; it felt like forever before the moment of impact, which would also mean the extinction of the glowing ash in the oily, iridescent water on the pavement. (*HL* 2.05, p. 74)

Ti-Jus as docked boat, and likewise the girl in the blue sweater during their brief love scene; or ships about to cast off, with the swirl of motion this implies around the hull . . .

But I'll come back to this episode later.

Disarm, Scuttle, Sink

Delivery of a wraparound skirt and a pantsuit becomes an occasion for a deadly rape . . . The events of the denouement don't change from one part of *Hoppla!* to the next. What do change, however, are the modalities of this denouement. The story stays the same, or nearly, but is differently developed, differently lit, and, of course, differently figured, so that the text is totally new each time and the three-part series is both varied and complementary, just as it satisfies the principles of repetition.

The cargo-ship denouement was fashioned in large part according to a triple stock image: a ship emptied of its crew and equipment; a ship riddled with irreparable leaks; a ship gone under—in other words, a ship successively disarmed, scuttled, sunk.

Result . . . In chapter 2.11, we find the hulk with the comb in the hallway at Madame Fenerolo's. At first he listens for "indecent sounds" coming from the bedroom. He experiences a moment of excitement, of gleeful agitation. Then, a change of mood, he leans glumly against the hummingbird-patterned wallpaper . . . He is the disarmed cargo ship, his slang playing the role of the equipment disembarked.

> Words crossed his mind, like *westerlies*, like *scuttling*, like *embark*, like *take on water*. He greeted each with a cynical mutter, holding them back an instant, then forsaking them altogether. *Westerlies* dropped in silence, tumbling down his sloping body, bouncing off the upper of one of his work boots; and *scuttling* and *embark* and *take on water* all rolled shakily across the carpet in turn, before coming to a stop, joining the ranks of an entire obsolete lexicon, rotting away in oblivion. (*HL* 2.11, p. 105)

Shortly thereafter, back in the living room, he performs several destructive acts, the last of which consists of ripping open a cushion. This disembowelment, a reenactment of what is concurrently taking place in the bedroom, is also a scuttling; the consequence will be an extended shipwreck—a shipwreck of the apartment, if not the whole Île-de-France region; shipwreck of the murderous hero and his accomplice; shipwreck of the prohibited but desirable manager; and finally shipwreck of the cargo-ship story that here comes to a close . . .

> As for the cushion, it was now less a cushion than an evisceration, a hole more than anything else, seemingly exposing the rest of the living room to the flow of some unspeakable catastrophe. For the moment, of course, there was nothing but cottony stuffing, whose gradual overspill hardly qualified as a flow at all; but the breach was bound

to widen, the tentative stream would become a surge, and once the kapok had poured out, an influx from deep within the inexhaustible elsewhere would follow—from the multiplicity of other apartment spaces and from the stairwell, then from the basement, the plumbing, and the standpipes, then from the suffocating cold of the outdoors and the night, all of which would come and lay siege to the manager's cozy three-room apartment. (*HL* 2.11, pp. 105–06)

JARGON

In the exercise of their profession, seamen use a jargon unintelligible to the outsider. They talk about *fothering* and *hawsers*, about *fairleads* and *hawse holes*, about *clinometers*. They use puzzling metaphors that sound obscene, such as *sling the slack* or *line the headstock*, as well as words such as *draught* and *headway*, used in their original sense. And where the landlubber would say *gangway*, *stop*, *pull*, or *take on water*, they say *board*, *avast*, *heave*, and *drink*.

Out of this authentic sailor-speak, I drew up a pseudo suburb-slang for part two of *Hoppla!* I diverted it in the same way as I did the botanical vocabulary in "The Coconut Palm." In some cases, I distorted it, and at all times associated it with other elements in the book.

Thus, when Ti-Jus and his buddies appear for the first time in the cargo-ship section, this also marks the first time we hear their jargon, different than that of "The Coconut Palm," but no less estranging, no less untranslatable.

The three boys said *bakker* instead of *back her*. They shortened *boatswain* into *bosun* or into simply *bos*, just as *Ti-Jus* became *Teejay* or *Teej* and *motherfucker* became *muff*.

"Let fly, muff, let fly!"

They spoke of *lining the windlass*, of *stowing* and *slackening the hawser*.

"Hey, TeeJay. Need some crew over there, or what?"

"All scuppers open! . . . " (*HL* 2.04, p. 72)

Bos, *Teejay*, and *muff*, result from a bricolage with only the remotest of cargo ship connotations. On the other hand, this pronunciation of *back her* as *bakker* would seem likely when an engineer is ordered to reverse the movement of the screws and urge the vessel astern; *let fly* in seaman-talk means to let go of a rope suddenly or all at once, just as *lining the windlass* means lifting the anchor by means of a pulley device, *stowing* means putting something in its place, *slackening the hawser* means easing the mooring cable, *to be short crew* means to lack personnel on board, and *scuppers* are pipes that drain water off the topside planking.

Another scene featuring this jargon, referred to earlier, in brief, is a tryst involving Ti-Jus and the girl in the blue sweater.

(During their secluded meeting, though they speak the same slang, the two young people have little to say to each other.)

They did make a promise to *unreeve*, to *ease off the main*, until the *anchor's aweigh* was pronounced. They kept their word and during the maneuver said "heave to," "slow as she goes," or "full speed ahead," accentuating the smooth stillness of the space around them with their noises, or else, at intervals, setting off a new onslaught—an uproar, even—in that same space, its silence bearing down on them. After which, she or he whispered "They'll be back any minute . . . we have to get out of here," though neither made a move to rise. With the tips of her fingers, the girl cleared a wisp of hair from her own face, a little sweat from the boy's. They kept repeating "We have to clear out of here," and finally did get up, because the regular occupants of the residence were in fact liable to arrive at any moment. (*HL* 2.08, pp. 88–89) Here we see how realistic features blend with cargo ship elements. The end of the quoted passage tends toward the realistic, whereas the lovers' choreography is all about cargo: the bodies locked in an embrace are the hull of a ship casting off; the space around them is the water of a dock, glassy everywhere except in the immediate proximity of the lateral propellers. Their jargon plays on shipping terms associated with the act of casting off: *to unreeve* is to unfasten a hawser from a ring or bollard; and when the all clear is given for the ship to cast off and leave harbor, *anchor's aweigh* is solemnly pronounced by the commander or the second in command. Lastly, *heave to*, *slow as she goes*, and *full speed ahead* pertain to variations in speed, and are spoken aloud by the helmsman and passed on to the engine room.

Though at times the jargon will conceal a secret metaphor—one which is in no way meant to be deciphered but rather inhabits a space that one might consider the text's private garden, its reticence—most of the time, it merely injects a bit of ordinary discourse with one or several unintelligible elements, either words whose cargo-ship/suburban usage has nothing to do with their original meaning, or words that have been so distorted as to become strange neologisms.

For instance, *Ro-Ro* (= Roll on/Roll off = a ship transporting in its hold or on deck vehicles, shipping containers, or rolling stock) or the expression "three sheets to the wind," when spoken by Ti-Jus or one of his buddies, become exclamations associated with feelings of frustration, even rage. "What's with this Ro-Ro?" shouts the hulk with the comb, in anger or feigned anger, when the doors of a parked car resist his attempts to pry them open (*HL* 2.05, p. 74). Or later, on the way to Vallon with Ti-Jus, when he loses his footing on the muddy ground, he swears "itchin'!" or "Three shits to the wind!"

And again, the nautical term *scuttlebutt* (= a barrel with a hole, used by sailors to drink from) gets diverted from its original meaning for purposes of cargo/street talk.

> This same soon halted, turned to his friends, and asked whether the sight of all those unguarded cars on an almost-empty street didn't want to make them *kick some scuttlebutt.* (*HL* 2.05, p. 74)

Or *swab*, derived from the obsolete *swabber* (= a mop used to clean the deck), from the Dutch word *zwabben*, meaning "to mop," a term used now almost exclusively in a marine context.

> Then he pounced on another umbrella. He asked the young couple sheltering underneath for a cigarette; from the girl in particular, he asked about the gold bracelet she wore on her wrist, and wondered whether she would agree to *swab the decks* or *buck up the baguette* on a handsome

young man like him. He persisted. It would be awfully nice
. . . All right, too bad—but the boyfriend would do in a
pinch, *buck up, swab*, wouldn't he . . . ? (*HL* 2.05, pp. 76–77)

Or again, the noun *hawsehole* (= a hole in the ship's bow for a
cable or chain to pass through) becomes a verb in suburban cargo-
speak.

He talks about the eleven-year-old kids, or not even eleven,
that hang out in gangs; about cats being stoned to death—
and not only stoned, and not only cats.
"You should have seen 'em *hawsehole* it!" (*HL* 2.10, p. 96)

This *hawseholing*, like the preceding examples, and indeed all
this cargo-ship jargon—let me reiterate—was devised with a twin
objective in mind: that it be untranslatable, and yet immediately
comprehensible. Challenging, perhaps, but not too hard to defend;
paradoxical, undoubtedly, but not much more so than many of our
daily gestures, glances and stutterings, or even literature itself, if by
literature we mean that territory where the play of language escapes
the constraints of everyday usage, and where, occurring as if at the
vanishing point of reason, it expresses the mystery of feeling in
terms that likewise affirm their obviousness.

The Centaur Way

Speed, endurance, the strength of a high-performance athlete, the power of an alpha male: such attributes give the centaur a certain advantage over an ordinary man. But how cumbersome that endless backbone dragging behind, and all those extra limbs! . . . And how ungainly that low-slung breast, those enormous flanks, those hindquarters, so muscle-bound and separate from the front part of the body! . . . And then, never to experience the grace and upright stature of the human, or worse, never to encounter a member of the opposite sex of one's species—for in this respect, I wanted to follow in the most ancient mythological tradition, according to which there are no female centaurs!

This same tradition, in fact, nearly always depicts the centaur as a ruthless, brutish creature, a ravisher ever on the prowl, feeding on raw flesh. In short, a monster to be kept at bay, outside civilized life, beyond culture, beyond the spoken word . . . Indeed, Homer, in Book II of the *Iliad*, refers to the centaurs as "ψηρας λαχυηεντας"— or in English, depending on the translation, something like "wild wooly beasts" or "long-haired brutes" or "hairy monsters."

Numerous Greek myths involve centaurs or establish their origins.

The most famous, illustrated on the Parthenon friezes, among others, tells the story of the battle between the Lapiths and the monstrous half-men-half-horses, which took place after the centaurs tried to ravish the bride at the wedding of Pirithous and Hippodamia. Equally famous is the tale of Heracles killing the centaur Nessus with a poisoned arrow while the latter was attempting to ravish

Deianira. Or the tale of the same Heracles facing off with a horde of drunken centaurs—Pholus, who along with Chiron is the other "good" centaur, is killed in the scuffle.

From a genealogical perspective, Zeus is said to have sought to unite with Dia by turning into a stallion. Dia was the wife of Ixion, king of the Lapiths, and father of Pirithous. Ixion is also said to have coveted Hera, and for this was punished by Zeus. The god first brought forth a cloud in the image of his wife—this illusion was to be Nephele, mother of all the centaurs except Pholus and Chiron—he then had the brazen Ixion tied to a burning wheel fated to spin forever in the heavens.

This is my basic stock material.

I will now show how, after the coconut palm and the cargo ship, the centaur was next to serve as an aid to the creation of various situations, a succession of ups and downs; characters, and both their nonverbal communication and their spoken language; and eventually a complete story—that of Judith revisited for a third and final time—not to mention, of course, the setting and atmosphere of the suburbs.

Four Boys as Centaurs
The cumbersome body
Though their secondary nature never actually becomes legible beneath their human personae, Ti-Jus and his buddies in the third installment of *Hoppla!* are in fact centaurs. They were already depicted as robust young men in "The Coconut Palm" and "The

Cargo Ship." In "The Centaur," their bulk is portrayed as even more unwieldy, and is deployed as such.

This is how the notion of four half-horses-half-men packed into a room, in association with the more realistic image of four large adolescent bodies, hanging out together, moodily, sparked the idea of emphasizing arms and legs in the following scene:

> Fallen silent once again, the four big boys would remain motionless for a time, their arms contorted into various positions, legs spread, crossed, bent at sharp angles, or stretched all the way out. The sum of so many appendages took on colossal proportions, bounded under the same ceiling and within the same four walls, such that it seemed no room could possibly contain a population that size; no living room, not even an entire suburban dwelling, whether it be an apartment or free-standing house. (*HL* 3.01, p. 110)

Likewise, it was the idea of him as centaur that made me situate at a certain point the hulk with the comb in a narrow underground pedestrian passage. I wanted him to behave like a horse whose headlong forward motion and massive size would turn such a narrow corridor into a frightening and dangerous place.

> Such an enormous, tumbling mass made the underground passage suddenly seem lacking in width, in height; in particular lacking any escape route, or at least a recess where any hapless passersby might have found shelter. The lateral walls and ceiling shook under the repeated impact of the hulk's work boots against the ground; daylight itself fled

before the recklessness of his assault . . . (*HL* 3.04, p. 124)

A further example. In the aftermath of their love scene, Ti-Jus and the girl in the blue sweater are looking out a window. I set them side by side so as to highlight their shared position—under siege (cf. Bethulia)—but also the discrepancy in their height.

[T]he two squatters behind the windowpane faced the outside world with the same stern brow, the same posture of disillusionment: twins, for one exceptional instant; their similitude more powerful than their gender difference or disparity in size. (*HL* 3.07, p. 144)

And shortly before, it was precisely the notion of an oversized Ti-Jus that determined the elements of the scene where the girl in the blue sweater finally catches sight of the boy she's been looking for:

He was far away; several passersby, as well as two or three stationary clusters of people, should all—according to the laws of perspective—have taken up more space in the *Maisonnaise*'s visual field. In her mind, however, he appeared to tower over everyone else in view, seemed so close that she reflexively withdrew her arm so as not to touch him prematurely. Then, having turned once again to her girlfriend—but her pelvis restive, legs itching to spring forward, and voice barely able to contain her euphoria: "Come have a look!" (HL 3.07, p. 142)

Let me emphasize here that, as is the case with the entire novel, although the passage above is indeed determined by the title motif, there are also other sources at work. It takes inspiration in part from scenes of the Annunciation so often painted by artists of the

Renaissance. (A book by Daniel Arasse entitled *L'Annonciation italienne* made clear to me how perspective came to be used in these works, particularly for the purpose of representing within the same space the incommensurability of human and divine figures.) Elsewhere, in the "Coconut Palm" section, there was a brief tableau of "girl discovering Ti-Jus" and falling for him immediately. This anonymous aspirant is given as representative of all girls.

> . . . and were one to approach him from a distance, she would scarcely have glimpsed the young man before she'd get excited, and, using the excuse of a girlfriend lagging behind, would turn around—"We're almost there!"—and by this ruse defer, for a suave, coquettish moment, the declaration that her euphoric face was burning to make to Ti-Jus. (*HL* 1.05, p. 21)

Whether in the coconut palm or the centaur version, these are new, suburban streetwise versions of the age-old theme of falling in love. Here and elsewhere in *Hoppla!*, these are also ways to conceive of representation starting with an object completely different from the one to be represented, not in denial of or contempt for that object, but rather, quite to the contrary, out of a desire to include it in a network of complicit realities—those that provide the foundation, let us say, of my personal mythology—and also the desire to give it a form that will have it appear at once completely familiar and irreducibly strange—a fragment of the ordinary world, of mundane human existence, and yet filled with more dreams, more musings, more memories and feelings than would be possible for consciousness to grasp, or, all the more, for any ordinary discourse to render in words.

The nonverbal: gait, pose, herding instinct

Besides being large and rather restless, centaurs, like horses, often kick and rear up, or strike the ground with their hooves. They can trot, gallop, walk, or go at an amble. Or if they're on a steep slope, in order to heave their heavy hindquarters to the summit, they must proceed by a series of strong, jerky movements.

This is why it happens that Ti-Jus and his posse dash off "in a headlong race" or are "jerk[ed] . . . suddenly to their feet"; that they "knock over plastic trash cans with a vengeance, or placekick the aluminum cans that littered the street." It is why, when someone's jaw gets in their way—or all of creation, for that matter—they "give out a brick-breaking karate chop"; and why, when they're hanging out together, they paw the ground at the foot of some endless housing block, or "[walk] in single file down the highway," obeying the herd instinct more closely in this section than in the previous two.

This is also why, in chapter 3.04, The Smoker and The Whistler take a footbridge. Thus, I was able to show them rising above the traffic, climbing steps or a ramp

> at a leisurely pace, striding forward purposefully nonetheless . . . spontaneously [heaving] themselves upward in a final effort to reach the top . . . (*HL*, p. 122)

And again, why Ti-Jus and the hulk with the comb, on their way to the Vallon neighborhood, walk together in step,

> bending a leg in unison and simultaneously stretching out the other, together raising a foot, extending it forward, pressing it to the ground, and so on, giving the impression of a single individual in motion. (*HL* 3.09, p. 151)

Here, to evoke two pairs of human legs, I described four horse legs, and the particular gait called ambling—aided by the fact that equine language speaks of a horse's *legs*, of its *shoulders* and *forearms*, thus sharing terminology with the human anatomy.

Elsewhere, I was reminded of a gesture often seen among horses in pasture involving one of their hind legs, and I adapted it to my young characters. Thus, in the scene evoked above, where the girl in the blue sweater finally tracks down Ti-Jus, the young man has

> [o]ne foot tucked under a buttock, sole and jeans pressed against a parked car . . . (*HL* 3.07, p. 142)

And in keeping with the same model, the three Parcae-girls of the denouement (I will address them further on) muse about how Ti-Jus and the hulk with the comb scrape the mud off the soles of their shoes, at once groom and horse; and then, how

> the large male bodies bend forward ever so slightly in perfect balance, each with a foot raised to about groin level, soles pointing up. (*HL* 3.10, p. 154)

Equine phallus

I made sure that the idea of this pelvic area, or more precisely, the equine phallus with which the centaur is equipped, was a frequent, if not constant, undercurrent of the text, and that occasionally the image would provide the core for an entire scene.

Here for example is how chapter 3.06 developed.

It had to do with evoking the Vallon Apartments in the centaur way: a tidier, plusher place than the Mermoz Projects; I sought to militarize the location a bit, as much for the Holofernes camp analogy as for the touch of realism it would add—hence, the multiple entryways, the doors with keypads, the intercoms, and the overt presence of the security guard. More distrustful and irritable than ever, in this section, this watchdog character was to be obsessed with the centauresque likeness of my four boys. To a couple of colluding residents of Vallon, he will verbalize his aversion to these creatures who he finds so unspeakable that he refers to them only as *they* and *those*. He will decry their physical appearance, how they "stood," how they "looked," and will harp incessantly on their nature as "pissers," repeating the word until it conjures up the catastrophic image of intruders shamelessly relieving themselves on the manicured lawns of the apartment complex.

Reflecting urban/suburban street reality as well as things equine, this act of desecration, however physiologically natural—urinating on the lawn—is perfectly suited to my goal. But if I lent it such importance in this scene, this is mostly because I wanted to evoke the image—designed nevertheless to remain subliminal—of the rutting stallion. To that end, I use the stream of steaming urine in the cold air, its tubular nimbus descending to the ground; and I mention the human "exposed phallus" only to conceal—or better to reveal—the very animal, very dark, very long horse penis that haunts not only the security guard but the text of this episode, both seemingly obsessed by the image.

Result:

> Or perhaps the intruding *all and sundry* would only include a few boys—but big ones, strong-limbed, hulking and violent enough to cause as much damage as a horde. They would wreck the lawn and the residential walkways with their

stampeding. They would overturn the cars parked in the visitors' lot, gleefully setting them ablaze. Or stationed at a certain distance from one another, in a random distribution, they would piss together, attempting at the same time to catch each other's eye and conversing merrily in their argot; and more concerned with their words than their deeds, a living insult to the local mindset, they would seem to be off in their own world, unconcerned by material existence and their own organisms, unmindful even of their own micturition, despite the cataract-like noise their urine would make when it struck the ground, as if to spite the cold, creating a long plume of vapor between the sprinkled ground and their bare penises. (*HL* 3.06, p. 136)

WOMAN AND RAVISHMENT
The feminine according to the centaur
Having postulated the nonexistence of female centaurs, I have in doing so posited women as doubly interesting in the eyes of the centaur: first of all, because they are entirely, exclusively human, and secondly, because they embody the gender of which the heterosexual stallions among the centaur species feel most deprived.

Hence the need for a partial redefinition of what is meant by *feminine* and *sexuality* in this third section of *Hoppla!*

I resolved early in the process that the crotch would be sexualized in a particular way here, not only as a genital zone, but as an aspect of the body that the centaur has lost. For the same reason, the hips, legs, feet and the mere image of anthropomorphic verticality are equally sexualized, as well as any position or movement involved in this upright state.

Thus, when at the SUMABA, Madame Fenerolo happens to mingle with the customers, she shines with a special brightness,

> not restricted to mere appearance but singularly present in all of her being, in her fullness, along with her legs, hips, waist, buttocks, crotch—all the parts of the body that go unseen beneath a skirt, of course, but that are truly there nevertheless, just as surely as her feet were truly in her pumps . . . (*HL* 3.03, pp. 117–18).

Or when the imagination of the customers reconstitutes the manager's body on the basis of voice alone, a voice that is broadcast over the store's intercom system announcing the upcoming opening of a new department and promoting the daily specials: "all frozen food on sale for one hour only, the homemade Creole-style blood sausages . . ."

> [T]he phonetic lengthening of *hour* in *for one hour* somehow conjured up the tapering of her legs; the syncopation of *eole* in *Creole-style* invoking the articulation of belly and thighs; or was it the cheerfulness, the bracing effect of *new department* that revived the way her two feet, all on their own, and as if making light of it all, had supported her body's upright linearity, defying gravity with each step: nimble, light, though resolute in their momentum and firmly planted on the ground at the moment of contact. (*HL* 3.03, p. 118)

Or again, Ti-Jus and his three buddies in search of girls, physically tormented by the idea of what they are seeking—and finally, the idea made flesh before their eyes . . .

> Four pairs of eyes would rush to fixate on the same passing crotch. Or alternatively, in a steadier kind of haste, they would scan the remainder of the creature, from top to bottom, as if to better appreciate her simple verticality. (*HL* 3.01, p. 112)

Throughout the *Centaur* section, verticality is valorized, sexualized in this manner—sometimes explicitly, other times implicitly—as are the slim extension of human legs and the way they move, bend, or hold the body upright in a delicate balance.

Figure of ravishment

Abduction, or better still, ravishment, is a fabled sort of concept, one might say, which has always struck the imagination. There was a certain consistency, if not inevitability, to including it as a major concept in my centaur fiction, and indeed it does play a key role in several episodes.

To begin with, here is how the passage from chapter 3.01, just cited above, continues, developing the fantasy that accompanies the sighting by Ti-Jus and his buddies of even the slightest trace of girl.

> And since the girl thus examined was so much a girl, from head to toe, the attraction she exerted would be fourfold, arousing the same violent bondage fantasy in each, the same fantasy of tying up this tangible being, getting her off balance,

lifting her up and carrying her off, her body arching helplessly, no part of her touching the ground. (*HL* 3.01, p. 112)

Likewise, Ti-Jus and the girl in the blue sweater are only playing at ravishment during their brief trysts.

Whether it was her or him that took the initiative or made the request, he lifted her off the ground and they moved from room to room, not at the pace of ordinary domestic business but literally racing, heedless of what might get knocked over in their path, fearing nothing that could have stopped them, as if henceforth all the space they wanted was theirs for the taking. Feather-light in the arms of the Mermoz boy, the girl was being held, supported, only by the back of her neck, an upper thigh, an armpit, with her limbs left free to resist the pull of gravity, her head floating, weightless. (*HL* 3.07, p. 143)

Here again, a painting provided me with a model, specifically a drawing by Picasso[4] depicting a woman being abducted by a centaur. If only I could have transposed into writing all that is tender, light, violent and colossal in this work—but also what is earthy, carnal, and yet weightless . . .

The concept of ravishment crops up again in the second to the last chapter, when the three little Parcae-girls posted at the entrance of

---

4 *The Rape*, 1920 (pencil, gouache and pastel). A reproduction of this drawing is found in the *Encyclopédie Universalis*, illustrating the entry "Drawing."

the Vallon Apartments watch the arrival of Ti-Jus and the hulk with the comb. Two of the girls are discussing the special properties of the two tall young men's shadows, while the third has her mind on other things.

> "They're going pass right by us," she predicts, excited at the prospect—and her girlfriends start teasing her: isn't she afraid of being knocked over, trampled? how would she like it if they kidnapped her . . . ? (*HL* 3. 10, p. 152)

And ravishment, to conclude, is of course present in the brutal act to which Madame Fenerolo will fall victim one final time.

> Ti-Jus lifts her up. "I'm going to . . . !" she resists. Ti-Jus prevents her from saying anything further. She feels dizzy. She grasps at whatever she can, but bumps into the wall, the wardrobe, the bed frame; and when the world has stopped spinning around her . . . (*HL* 3.11, p. 159)

This part of the narrative refers to an implicit scene featuring the manager as involuntary rider, perched precariously on a mount whose "spirit," in these circumstances, comes not from any angelic zeal or amorous desire, but from some fiendish drive to exterminate.

Dissemination of the Centaur

I didn't want this system to be too rigid, nor was I eager for the centaur, appearing as such, to take up too much room and edge out the principal material of my suburban novel (i.e., the suburbs themselves, and everything about the story of Judith that was, from my perspective, appealing, disturbing, unnerving, and, in a word, inexhaustible). This is why the application of the centaur assumes a wide range of fanciful forms, going beyond and sometimes contradicting the simple formula of Ti-Jus + buddies = herd of man-horses, extending its influence to a variety of characters, settings, situations, more or less overtly contaminating the narrative lexicon.

Equine aspects even penetrate the minds of Ti-Jus and his friends.

This is the case as early as the first chapter of section three, when tormented by the "idea of girl," and having been practically struck dumb, the four boys have faces with "sockets widened in pain and eyes blazing with fury" (*HL* 3.01, p. 109).

Likewise, shortly before they take the pedestrian overpass mentioned earlier, Smoker and Whistler are (implicitly) depicted as head-to-toe horses—walking with blank stares, snorting or shaking themselves in the cold . . .

> A vicious watchdog could start barking, rain could come pouring down, or a gust of winter air bring them the odor of gasoline or the smells of woodland undergrowth, and the two hikers would still continue obliviously along their path, as if deprived of their senses; the invariable brightness of their eyes betraying no one particular inner state any more than another—inebriation no more than passion, or lack of sleep, or any particular feeling besides emptiness. They walked along absentmindedly, each letting out his breath from time to time: spasmodic, like a tic. The Whistler would shoot a hoot-like whistle into the air; The Smoker would rock his head back, sometimes expelling smoke from his mouth, sometimes just steam. (*HL* 3.04, p. 122)

And as for the hulk with the comb, when in chapter 3.07 he displays his general hostility to the world, this is also in a totally equine manner, since not only does he stomp on the ground "as though trying to split open the asphalt," but "chest thrust forward," he "chew[s] up" the horizon on all sides.

On the other hand, though the double nature of the centaur body often determines this or that gesture, posture, or outfit adopted by one or another of my four adolescents, the same basic image was also applicable to characters depicted as far less bestial, or indeed not antisocial in the least.

This is notably the case in chapter 3.02 which takes place at the SUMABA. The young apprentice butcher, marveling at how human his own hands are, and sensually running the strands of a lashed curtain through his fingers, as one might the leafy branches of some tree, is indeed a kind of satyr (though the satyr is usually half-goat, half-man, it is sometimes half-horse in the Dionysian procession). And the supermarket customers themselves merge with their grocery carts to become "half-figures" whose human aspect stops at waist level.

But the tool of the centaur was put to its best use in describing the suburban landscape. For instance, the notion of a file of horses treading back and forth over the same terrain, eventually wearing a path into the ground, led me to evoke "the paths worn by the repeated passage of RER rail-commuters" (*HL* 3.01, p. 112)—paths which, by the way, can in fact be found around many suburban train stations, the result of the sort of spontaneous, daily habit that seems to take pleasure in outwitting urban planners.

Elsewhere, while Whistler and Smoker are standing on the pedestrian overpass, a scene mentioned earlier, the suburban landscape is described from a thoroughly equine perspective . . . Or there is the moment when the security guard at the Vallon Apartments imagines in horror that the shrubbery planted on his precious lawn has been festooned triumphantly with bits of detritus floating in the wind:

> newspapers, bits of rag, plastic bags, and even long filaments of jute or of fiberglass, each clump looking like a raw chunk of scalp. (*HL* 3.06, p. 136)

These "clumps," these "long filaments," refer directly to horsehair from the manes or tails of real horses, which gets torn off and tangled in the branches of trees and bushes.

Elsewhere still, the girl in the blue sweater and her girlfriend trying to locate the Mermoz housing projects have just arrived at a major intersection. As always, I combined two apparently contradictory concerns: on the one hand, that of producing a precise rendering of a certain kind of place, of putting into words the feeling of space that such a place engenders; and on the other hand, that of making use of the centaur tool. Hence the dual design of the two teenage girls who, in the passage in question, are simultaneously on foot and on horseback, compelled to "skirt the traffic flow, seek out a stepping stone" (*HL* 3.07, p. 141).

Finally, just as the coconut palm and cargo ship were previously, the centaur gets applied to traffic jams, a quintessential feature of the suburban landscape.

Once again, the process consisted of layering the realist and centaur material upon one another. In other words, firstly: vehicles in great number, traffic reduced to a crawl or gridlocked over several

kilometers, the usual passive-aggressive mix among the drivers—
their sudden impulses to change lanes, the revving of their motors
and the attendant bursts of exhaust fumes and episodic horn honking. And then, secondly: a herd of wild horses in a procession both
long and compact, the exhaustion of the animals, their machinelike
march, with the occasional beast splitting off from the herd—for the
horse is a skittish animal, subject to phobias that sometimes make
them start at the mere sound of a rolling pebble or a mere glint off
water—accompanied by an animal breaking wind or another expel-
ling dung . . . In this regard, and perfectly timed, I was reminded of
the French word *fumée*: in addition to its more common usage, designating exhaust fumes, it can also mean, when in the plural, wild
animal droppings that are useful in tracking down game.

Result:

> Car door to car door, bumper to bumper, vehicles of all
> makes, models, and sizes were creeping forward, when
> they weren't completely gridlocked. Occasionally, an ex-
> haust pipe would roar or explode with impatience. Else-
> where, due either to a half-asleep motorist suddenly roused
> from his torpor, or to a phobic reaction to the shimmering
> of some puddle on the blacktop, a car would suddenly pull
> out of line. This would set off a chain reaction of disorderly
> conduct, accompanied by a concert of car horns. But the
> disturbance would be short-lived, as if in the surrounding
> gloom the drivers were even more keenly aware than in day-
> light of the indecency of their noises. Reduced once again
> to rumbling engines, alternatively idling or gearing up,
> gleaming with rain, haloed in fumes and the steam released

continuously by their hot metal into the cold air, the long cortege of vehicles seemed resigned to an endless migration under the russet, rain-soaked suburban sky. (*HL* 3.03, p. 119–120)

THE CENTAUR POINT OF VIEW

Narration

The SUMABA has just closed for the night. Most of its employees have already left, and Madame Fenerolo is in the vast, deserted parking lot, walking out to her car where Bessie is standing and waiting for her. The manager then turns around, and at a distance, raising her voice slightly, instructs her night-watch team to line up the grocery carts and chain them securely.

This very brief scene—a few lines—occurs in each of the three *Hoppla!* sections, creating three variations, the third of which is as follows:

"Good and tight!" she shouted, emphasizing each syllable, like the execution of a figure-skating jump with its takeoff and landing. (*HL* 3.03, p. 119)

There are centaur resonances in this bit of narrative, not only with regard to the jump reference (referencing, that is, an athlete or a horse), but also and especially in that it pertains to the fascination exerted upon the man-horse by the bipedal nature and vertical posture of the human body, the female human in particular, as is borne out by the remainder of the passage.

In another chapter, the narration comes to espouse at length—and close to explicitly—the centaur point of view. This is due to the presence of the same pronoun WE that was previously bound up with coconut palm and then with cargo ship. Early in chapter 3.08, the narration switches into focalized first person, exposing how much the speaker/subject WE dreads certain utterances that he feels stirring mutely within.

> Should this utterance happen to escape, suddenly inhab-iting the open air, resounding in our own voice, we would fail to recognize it, would grow afraid, feel ashamed, as though we had forgotten how to use language; or else, if we were able to puzzle out the meaning of those sounds, we would find that we had been reproducing the very same words that reveal us to be rough beasts, compounding our shame—and the fear that would soon moisten our skin and make our hair sticky would indeed bring out our most ani-mal odors. (*HL* 3.08, p. 145)

Here, two remarks are in order:

1. This WE, whose narrative focalization is nearly always (and only nearly) identified explicitly as the centaur, is certainly closer to Ti-Jus and his buddies than to any other character. And yet, it does not establish a classic subjective first-person narrative. First of all, because it is presented as something exceptional. Secondly, because it is first-person *plural*, a referent to some collective abstraction, and not to a presumably thinking, feeling individual. And thirdly, be-cause all psychological causality is banned from *Hoppla! 1 2 3*, a novel where, in imitation of Racine's tragedies or of epic poetry, the characters are mere designated agents, excluded from the decision-making process—whether the hand of fate or the novelist's outline—as to what will inexorably come to pass.

2. For me, adopting the centaur's point of view meant sticking as closely as possible to my stock material, being ever mindful of it

in the most concrete terms and treating it as if there were no referent other than itself, such that my fiction, as it deployed in its own
space, would have enough breathing room and not be strangled by
the rigid confines of some ideological framework. Formal styliza-
tion, YES—since this is where novels are born—but dogmatic simplification of the world, exacerbated by an arbitrary assignment of
values, NO. Naturally, when it came to collective reality, like everyone else, I had and continue to have my personal likes and dislikes,
my convictions, my disgusts, my doubts, all of whose role in the
Hoppla! enterprise was far from trivial. Naturally as well, my centaur
was and remains the possible image of quite a few things: the beast
at the core of the human soul, the savagery of civilization, or the
scapegoat, and with him, all outcasts, all exiles—exiled from society,
from the opposite sex, from ideals, from ideas, from speech, from
tenderness . . . But however long the list, and whatever its contents,
to my mind the centaur still had to fulfill its centaur-ness, first and
foremost. To resist being reduced to what it would possibly come to
represent. To exceed any signification.

Stated otherwise: I have not written a moral fable, but a novel,
that is, a work of fiction whose form I set out to personalize and
master, while not intending to reduce or control its meaning. In the
latter case, this meant taking risks. In the former, exercise of freedom. And it's the writer's basic duty never to deviate from either
obligation.

Antiquity in the tropics
Though it goes unnamed in the *Hoppla!* suburbs, the centaur retains
a bit of the aura of its antique Greco-Roman origins.

Throughout the novel, without any hint of incongruity, one comes across "a sorrowful omen" or "divining powers," an "aegis," a "Chimera," or "Night Itself." Television becomes "the wisdom of a soothsayer"; elsewhere, entrails reveal the future, while in the final chapters, the three Parcae-girls (I'll return to them) are more Parcae than ever. Prior to this point, Madame Fenerolo had already come in out of the rain, soaked to the skin, but in imitation of Venus Anadyomene, rising from the sea.

> To everyone—customers and staff alike—who saw her coming back through the door of the SUMABA in this state, not only did she bear no resemblance whatever to the disheveled woman one might have expected under these circumstances, but she was all smiles, her complexion refreshed by the cold, and her figure embellished, as though blossoming after contact with her primal element. (*HL* 3.03, p. 117)

And by chapter 3.01, Dryads, Nereids and other nymphs have started making appearances in the south suburbs.

> [T]he four boys would avidly watch the passing traffic or scrutinize the endless façade of some apartment block, searching outside themselves for the very thing, the idea of which they'd been experiencing inside themselves for so long, anxious to visualize it, at last incarnate, emerging from some automobile or masonry, as in ancient times some ideal creature might have emerged from a tree, the sea, a river, or a rock, come to bequeath upon passersby— be they men or gods—the vision of a tangible beauty. (*HL* 3.01, p. 111–112)

*

But in association with this trace of Antiquity, the centaur also exudes the persistent memory of the tropics.

All three sections of *Hoppla!* share in this phenomenon. All contain a number of invariable features that contribute to this diffuse tropical atmosphere. For instance, Ti-Jus with his "wooly hair," the family name "Deux-Rivières" (Trois-Rivières being a town in the French Antilles), the first names Bessie and Celestin, more typical of the French tropics, but also the African resonances of the store name SUMABA (which is simply an acronym for **Su**per**ma**rket of **Ba**gneux), and even the suggestion of the Caribbean buried in the name of the region itself, Île-de-France.

Particularly in "The Centaur," mention is made of a "backwater," of a "climbing vine," both of which resonate with the hurricanes Bessie keeps recalling, or the wild animals "gather[ing] to quench their thirst in the brown water." The chapter also suggests the charm a language acquires when colored by a certain accent, enough to "make a commonplace sound like a pearl of wisdom"; there is also talk of the banks of the Seine at Ris-Orangis and of a place that Ti-Jus discovered there,

> an interesting nook from which poles, buildings, and indeed all signs of human existence were concealed by the blackish vegetation on either shore, where the river one could see flowing through the virgin landscape looked like some other river, Île-de-France some other isle, in some other country . . . (*HL* 3.07, p. 139)

Finally, even before the appearance in the narration of the centaurlike WE mentioned earlier, a totally tropical WE of recent immigrant origins becomes manifest as follows:

(*Smoker and Whistler are gazing out upon a broad
suburban panorama.*)
But the two boys paid little attention to the landscape, any
more than they had at any other time, clearly indifferent
to the world of the senses, or perhaps identifying so strongly
with what made up their everyday environment that they
felt no need to visualize it in order to experience its presence, nor indeed to perceive it through any of their senses—
just as we need not actually see the sun of this dry season
weave light and shadow at our feet, nor do we need to see
the rainy season's showers pelt the brownish-red puddles
along the boulevard and varnish the termite mounds, nor
hear its frenzied clamor strafing our roofs, because we always keep alive within us—though perhaps at the very back
of our minds—the past presence of those partition screens,
reddish laterite soils, and corrugated tin. (*HL* 3.04, p. 123)

JARGON

Borrowings of various sorts—*détournement*, distortion, creation,
word breakdown, the same processes I put to work for the two previous sections' jargons are also implemented in centaur slang. For
this last section, however, proper names issuing from ancient Greek
mythology accounted for a large share of the stock material, and I
made more use than elsewhere of a kind of back slang, applied often
to a vocabulary having to do with horses or sex.

Thus Nephele (from the Greek, meaning "cloud") who is, I reiterate,
the mother or grandmother of all centaurs) + Pholus (exceptional

twice over as a good centaur and conceived by Silenus with a nymph of the ash groves) + a bit of English + a little tweaked Sardinian dialect, all these come together in association to create the following:

> To this signal, the friends responded with the same "We're out of here," this time in the affirmative, adding a couple of variants, from "Bye-bye *phaï-laï*," to "Let's go, *pholo*," including "Lead the way, *phélé*, we're behind you!" (*HL* 3.05, p. 126)

Or Hippodamia (the fiancé that the centaurs wanted to abduct) + Eurytos (or Eurytion, the first of the abductors) =

> (*The four Mermoz boys, having arrived at the Évry Bowling Alley, are conversing a bit with The Gardeners, a rival gang.*
> *A fight will break out later.*)
> Various bits of news were thus exchanged, greeted with "uh-huh" and "hip!" with "'*rytos*" with "'*poddamia*," half smug, half skeptical. (*HL* 3.05, p. 127)

Likewise, the names of Dia and Ixion will get mixed into the slang, as they are, with no modification whatsoever.

Modification does take place, however, whenever I use back slang or any other more or less standard process.

Thus "stud," the breeding stallion, and "nicker," from a special use of the verb *to nick*, meaning to cut the tendons at the root of a horse's tail to make the tail stand up, combine into the oddly resonant *stud nicker*. The Évry Bowling Alley sign inspires *ever-bowl*. From Chiron, the wise centaur, (pronounced *ki-* like *kite*), and via *chiro-*, Greek for "hand," the vaguely lewd *kyroballs*. From Homer's "wild, hairy beasts," I extracted "furry," which is back-slanged into *reefur*, with both drug and marine ("reef") resonances. From

"Alcides," another name for Heracles, I derived a simple common noun; from archery, I borrowed the old verb *to fletch* (to equip an arrow with feathers), all combining to produce this first appearance of centaur slang in 3.01:

> They would use words of their own coinage, such as *Furry* and *Reefur*, *fletch* and *fletching*—"You're fletching my alcides shaft, huh Reefur?" (*HL* 3.01, p. 110)

Likewise, when I needed to add some dirt to the centaur jargon, *mule* became *lemu* and *throatlatch* shortened to *tlatch* to produce:

> [T]hey would call him *mule* or *lemu* or *throatlatch* or just *tlatch*, the way other friends in conversation might call one another prick or jerk. (*HL* 3.07, p. 138)

Or, in search of more blasphemous swear words, I thought of archaic ones such as *gadzooks*, or *gosh darn it* and *dang blast it* (both derived euphemistically from *God damn it*), or *zounds* ("God's wounds") and *odds bodkins* ("God's body"). Taking inspiration from these models, I substituted Nephele (the cloud goddess) for God, and shortened the name to *nephe* or *phele*, and with the standard *ho* from *whore*, to produce *nepheho* and *pheleore*, while *plasma* was an anagram for "palsam" in the archaic French expression *palsambleu* (a corruption of "par le sang de Dieu" or "by the blood of God"), reordered into *plasmaphele*.

Indeed, the slang curse *plasmaphele*, which appears in chapter 3.04 after being foreshadowed in "The Cargo Ship,"[5] will figure as the closing word of the centaur section, and hence the final word of the

---

5   Ti-Jus is seen there walking to the Vallon Apartments in solemn silence, condensing within himself "the entirety of his own story, from *Radio messages* to *plasmaphele*." (*HL* 2.09, p. 94)

novel—which thus ends with a covert reference to the maternal image that, no less covertly, has shaped the entire triptych.

But why this constant secrecy, raised here to the nth power? What's the use in introducing so many elements into a novel that will only prove unfathomable to the reader? . . .

I persist in believing that motive and usefulness underlie the same conviction championed in such an exemplary manner by Erich von Stroheim who, while filming *The Wedding March*, demanded of an extra, lost in the remotest background of a crowd scene, that he wear a pair of gloves that could never possibly be visible to any movie-goer; or when he insisted to his producers that the bell cords in a fake palace (this was still the silent era) should actually make bells ring. Thus demonstrating that even though art's special effects aim at creating an illusion, they are still concerned exclusively with the rigorous precision of their devices, as if each such device must bear the responsibility of producing all the power of the work, or of transmitting its truth via the lavish transformation of authentic desires and wounds into entirely fictive passions.

Pleasant Surprises

During the novel-writing process, to the author's great astonishment, he sometimes discovers that the hand of fate has worked in his favor. Or at least, this is his impression when, upon rereading his text for the umpteenth time, he suddenly apprehends an unexpected meaning or connotation, a stubborn echo of his own personal story, or a resurgence of some implicit theme he believed to have buried deep in the subtext; and likewise, while doing some research, he comes across a word he never knew existed, but which he immediately recognizes as the one he needed to complete a certain sentence.

The surprise elicited by such realizations or discoveries brings on a brief moment of intellectual giddiness, followed soon after by a more lasting satisfaction: that of being the recipient of an auspicious sign, one attesting that the machinery operating in the novel's workspace is functioning well enough to make up for memory lapses and mental blocks, and to breathe into the text the kind of emotion that springs from memory as well as the special jubilation that accompanies the intelligence of language.

I experienced a few of these pleasant surprises while writing *Hoppla! 1 2 3.*

Sagittarius, hazelnut trees, and mosaic parquet

For examples of involuntary homonymity and unexpected resonances, the preceding pages have hinted at "fellate" in *phele*, at "fletching" in *fletch* or a certain insular exoticism in *Île-de-France*. Equally serendipitous was the discovery that *plasma* was an anagram for "palsam," which, as I demonstrated earlier, doubles the dose of blood delivered by the word, rather than attenuating it, albeit with a mischievous and seemingly inevitable insistence.

There were others, all meaningful to me, though not of equal implication or weight.

For instance, it took me several years to realize how closely linked centaur and cargo ship had become in my personal symbolic field. At the outset of my project, or shortly before it assumed its definitive form, I had considered adding to the three title motifs a couple more: BALUSTER, for example, and SHOE. It wasn't long before I abandoned these. They must not have been deeply rooted enough in my psyche, or else they lacked the requisite age and heft. The three others, however, have accompanied me since childhood. They so affected me that they have always found their way into my books. And yet, one thing was still bothering me: coconut palms and cargo ships, with their suggestions of travel, faraway shores, the high seas, etc., seemed to share a common thematic thread, whereas centaur seemed like an outsider in the trio of section titles! I figured that this incongruity should be turned into an advantage, if possible—that of interrupting the all too obvious unity of the first two motifs, whose cliché value was relevant only to the extent that I might attempt to subvert it . . . Even so, my unease persisted. And then, coconut, cargo, centaur, those three Cs seemed to be trying to mean something, although to my mind, this triple initial was purely accidental. Clearly, my motifs were starting to trouble me.

And then, one day, as it happens to all of us every so often, I was suddenly struck by the obvious, something that hadn't exactly fallen into oblivion, nor fully lost its character as self-evident, but rather had sunk, simply, into an inactive state, as if slumbering in my consciousness. Centaur and cargo, I was to realize that day, were two realities that had been referring back and forth to one another for quite some time already. For I was the child of a certain ship, a cargo ship called *The Sagittarius*—a name that points back to none other than Chiron the centaur, become a heavenly constellation. This ship was as much a part of my education, cultivation, and protection as all manner of coconut palms had been.

(Surprise within this surprise: writing the name of that cargo ship from out of the past has just opened my ears to yet another connection I failed to spot: in the words *sagette*, *ça jette*, or *sagetter*, I had never before noticed *Sagittarius*!)[6]

*

A similar coincidence occurred with the word *coudrier*.

The hulk with the comb, in the tenth chapter of "Centaur," is going along with Ti-Jus to the Vallon Apartments, when out of nowhere he evokes the "Coudriers Projects." It eventually comes out that *coudrier* is a less frequently used word in French for *noisetier*, or hazelnut tree, and that in the past, the word was pronounced in two syllables (*cou-drier*), and, finally, that it has become difficult to articulate the word that way today.

---

6 The verb *sagetter* in the French original is one of the slang terms used by the Ti-Jus and his friends, an archaic term having to do with arrows, and translated by the specialized term *fletch* in the English version of *Hoppla! 1 2 3*, which refers to equipping an arrow with feathers. *Ça jette* or "it throws/hurls," is a homonym for *sagette*. —Translator's Note.

I had several reasons, or at least thought I did, to introduce this random word.

1. This tree's branches are used to make canes and switches, perfect for "The Centaur."

2. On one or two other occasions in preceding chapters, the hulk with the comb has already outed himself as an unlikely lexicologist. His remarks about the word *coudrier* constitute a further variation. Moreover, it suited my purpose to take an opposite view of the clichéd streetwise thugs of these urban fringes, as well as to break with the mimetic traditions of reported speech in narrative fiction.

3. I also found it fitting, as a counterpoint to the numerous other linguistic modes in the text, to let the archaic pronunciation resound: *cou-drier*, in two syllables.

It was only after the novel had been completed, I believe, or in any case a long while after I had placed this *coudrier* in the text, that it all clicked: One of the places I spent my teenage years in was a housing project. I hadn't forgotten it, since at several points it had served as a model for the Mermoz Projects. But between that place of my youth and the word *coudrier*, I had never before made the slightest connection, even though its name—probably borrowed from an earlier topography, referring to the area's former woodlands—was (and still is, I assume) the "Bas-Coudrais" [*sic*], or Lower Hazelnut Groves, Projects.

*

In the Bas-Coudrais Projects, the parquet floor was set right onto concrete slabs. It was made up of short slats assembled five-by-five to form squares in a kind of checkerboard pattern—which was then called "mosaic parquet."

It took me a long time, and I was all the more satisfied thanks to this delayed reaction, to hear in the apposed noun *mosaic* the name of Moses (as in "Mosaic Law"), as this meant that, unbeknownst to me, the story of Judith and its heroine's Jewishness had slyly emerged to the surface of the text *Hoppla!*

Teej, hispines, *and the etymology of* metro

It's in the cargo ship section that Ti-Jus is nicknamed *Teej* for the first time, a homonym for the French word "tige," meaning the stem, stalk, or shaft. In my mind, rather than an extension of some slang, it was simply a whim, like the one that was soon to introduce the nicknames "Smoker" and "Whistler," or to ratify the descriptor "hulk with the comb." It therefore came as a pleasant surprise when, in addition to the sexual connotation implicit in "shaft"—and, practically speaking, this early reference to the centaur's physique—I could also hear coconut-palm jargon intruding into cargo territory. Indeed, foresters and botanists refer to "stalks" and "shafts" rather than "trunks," especially when it is a matter of stipes, as is the case with *Palmae.*

Teej, Ti-Jus . . . How is it that throughout the more than two years that it took me to write the coconut palm section, I was never able to make that connection?

*

Just as it often happens in real life, throughout *Hoppla!* a kind of sexual pressure made itself felt, sometimes silently, other times in discursive allusions or lexical connotations. The centaur jargon in particular features not only some lewd terms borrowed from everyday speech, but an even larger amount of less predictable crudeness. Hence the largely anticipated *dickhead* or *asshole* mingle with *buck mount*, *Reefur*, or *vaysh* from *vayshun*, derived from "aggravation," all inserted into a stretch of stunning inarticulateness.

At this point, I have to go back to October 2000. I was finishing up the centaur section at that time. "The Coconut Palm" had been completed four years previously. I would go back to it only on occasion for the odd correction, adjustment, tweak . . . One detail, however, remained exceptional. Upon her first encounter with Ti-Jus and the other Mermoz boys on the Paris-Corbeil commuter train, the girl in the blue sweater went into a kind of screaming fit. Before getting to "I'm gonna be weaving your *coir!*" and the aftermath, referenced earlier, she began in this earlier draft raging at the overly insistent boys with: "You're weeviled, weeviled, get it?"

I was hoping to replace this pseudo-verb *to weevil* with a more technical word, so as to make the slang more specifically and covertly coconut.

A specialized reference work supplied me with the name of a family of weevils particularly harmful to *Cocos Nucifera*: HISPINES . . . With "pine" pronounced in French like "peen" as in "penis," I couldn't have come up with anything better. Science and triviality combine into a broad, potentially dubious term, likely to be used in verbal abuse. Again, the science is pure coconut, whereas the trivial overtones stem from the implicit rudeness of the angry teenage girl, but undoubtedly even more from the way the word ends in *pine*—a syllable thus present in the coconut-palm slang that contributes to its brutal sexualizing, just as, in the French text, the final syllable of *lapine* (female rabbit) and *tapine* (streetwalker) are dropped to create *lap* and *tap*, whose excised portions, by their invisibility, make the words sharper, semantically less comprehensible and therefore more threatening.

*

Among other short texts whose purpose is to enlighten, or to reactivate through fresh representations the autobiographical underpinnings of *Hoppla! 1 2 3*, there is an anecdote in the last section of *this* book entitled METRO. There, I first relate a scene I actually experienced, linked to the fact that long before the word *canary* referred to a bird, it meant for me an earthenware pot. I then evoke the many meanings of the word *metro*: the "metro" in the sense of urban mass-transit vehicle or network; the old "metro" franc, the reference currency for the French Pacific islands CFP and African CFA francs prior to the creation of the euro; or a person coming out to the territories from the metropole, as opposed to the native, or indigenous population . . . All of which culminates in the final formulation of this anecdote: "distant and ambivalent French motherland." This phrase seeks to get across a personal relationship to one's country of origin wherein foreignness and distrust are pitted against familiarity and affection. The motherland leads necessarily to the mother—and here, motherland somehow echoes with the *plasmaphele* of the centaur slang.

Though this anecdote had already been written, filed away, and all but forgotten, as I was looking up some other word in a dictionary, I came across *metropolis*. And more precisely, my eyes zoomed in on the etymology *mêtêr* (mother) + *polis* (city). *Polis*—well even without being a Hellenist, I knew that one. But *mêtêr*, not at all—I had never thought to trace *metro* back to *mater*! . . .

I thought myself so clever by finishing my text with *motherland*. In fact, I had simply, naively, repeated my title—or conversely, with *metro* I had accidently prefigured the closing words of my text.

The Parcae-girls, shadows, and the gum-chewer

The Parcae-girls are characters who, in each of the three sections of my triptych, appear only in the tenth and next-to-last chapter, that is, at the start of the denouement. They are standing at the entrance to the Vallon Apartments when Ti-Jus and the hulk with the comb arrive on the scene; and while the events in the manager's apartment are taking place, events that since Biblical times were bound to take place, outdoors the girls are taunting the grouchy security guard, or they are patiently awaiting the return of the boys, relaxed and feeling at home in the cold winter night air.

In "The Coconut Palm," nevertheless, they make only a fleeting appearance. I had no idea, in fact, while writing this first section, that the girls would become more important in the subsequent ones, and that they had already assumed their role as allegories of death. All I had wanted to do, at the final turning point of the story, was to place three young girls in the path of Ti-Jus as a counterpart to the first time we encounter the young man.

Perhaps it was his halo of wooly hair, his aerial silhouette, and a certain solar luster emanating from his person that all made Ti-Jus so popular with the girls. Willingly, women or young girls would allow themselves to come into contact with his skin, pressing their dresses or jeans, their under-garments, their bare flesh to it fearlessly . . . (*HL* 1.05, p. 21)

And then, the young girls from the Mermoz Projects just watch the two boys walk into the distance. Three girls placed on the Vallon side provide the opposite vantage point, which makes the daredevil crossing of Avenue de Paris—a raised multilane road with heavy traffic—a clearer and more decisive move toward the denouement.

Later on, as the cargo ship story is reaching the same decisive turning point, I felt my trio of little girls could play a role of utmost importance by bringing to the scene of rape and murder the counterpoint of a presence both childlike and funerary, fraught with cruelty, but also marked by lightness and mischief. At that point, I still had in mind to create some girls in the cargo-ship mode (whether little tugboats escorting a ship, or seagulls floating on the water's surface), before coming up with the idea of their being the Parcae.

In the third section, however, I knew from the outset what role my three girls were going to play. They share with the centaurs an origin in Antiquity, and thus would feel at home with them. In addition, they fit right into my view of the novel's trajectory as moving progressively into the tragic register. Thus, the third and final section of *Hoppla!* is where the analogy between the girls and the Parcae is the most salient, the most emphatic. But, at the time, I didn't realize just how much. And this was the occasion for two more pleasant surprises.

1. In chapter 3.10, while Ti-Jus and the hulk with the comb are descending the embankment of Avenue de Paris to get to the Vallon Apartments, the three girls are watching the two large young men from below, and in particular, the moving outline of their shadows on the ground. These images, says the text, seem "as though under threat by the wind." And a few lines later:

> One of the young girls claims that these particular shadows have special qualities. In addition to being impervious to pain, they're nimble, almost imperceptible, and therefore harmless. At which the nonchalant girl shrugs: "All shadows are like that . . . !" (*HL* 3.10, p. 152)

Why these shadows? And where did my ideas about them come from? . . .

At this point in the story, I wanted a scene that would announce the fateful denouement while offering a brief respite—a little peace, perhaps, and some of that gentleness of which the novel would soon be in short supply.

It so happened that I had taken some notes on a work by the painter Konrad Witz, discovered five or six years earlier in Strasburg, at the *L'Œuvre Notre-Dame* museum. I had also copied out an extract from Roland Barthes's *Empire of Signs*.

The painting dates back to 1444. It depicts Mary Magdalene and Saint Catherine inside a church, a long oblique space, more or less empty, broken up only by the columns and pillars of the nave and the shadows they cast, alternating with light spaces on the floor and walls. The shadows in Konrad Witz's works, and especially this one, have always appeared exceptionally gentle to me. I had been wanting to draw on this feeling for quite some time.

As for the Barthes text, which deals with Japanese Bunraku dolls, he evokes qualities that "the dreams of ancient theology granted to the redeemed body, i.e., impassivity[7], clarity, agility, subtlety . . ."

This is why the three little girls in "The Centaur" conduct this debate about shadows. Ti-Jus and the hulk with the comb attain "redeemed" bodies (though stopping short of clarity), consistent with the angelic nimbus ascribed to at least one of them elsewhere . . . Yet, unbelievably, I organized and wrote this passage neither hearing nor seeing its best, simplest, most obvious justification: all this "shadow" talk suited the Parcae in that it was talk about the dead.

2. At the end of the cargo-ship section, the Parcae-girls are right below Madame Fenerolo's windows. As explicitly *girls*, they are waiting for their recent crushes, the two big young men, to come back down. As *implicitly* Parcae, they are on the scene to cut the thread of someone's life—and since there is also something of the Furies in these Parcae, they most likely will not be letting the rapist-murderer off the hook anytime soon . . . But on the other hand, as I've already said, after playing the tugboats that escort Ti-Jus and the hulk with the comb, they end up as seagulls floating on the water. What constitutes the water, as established in an analogy already deployed in the first chapter, are the roofs and hoods of the cars parked in the apartment complex visitors' lot. One of the girls, in the closing gesture of the cargo-ship section, bends over and disappears for a moment, concealed by the vehicles.

----

7 Impassivity in the archaic sense of the word, i.e. insusceptibility to pain.

Perhaps an itch on her calf, her foot. Or maybe the feeling that one of her socks was twisting around her ankle had begun to annoy her. She had undertaken to scratch the itch, to hike up the sock. But once one or the other gesture had been accomplished, she resurfaced into the carscape, her lips rounded to produce a huge chewing-gum bubble . . . (*HL* 2.11, p. 106)

I will address the end of the sentence later on, as well as the main reason for the bubble. The fact remains that bubblegum appears here because I needed a bubble—if only to stand in for the fish in the beak of the diving seagull.

In the centaur section, though no longer a seagull, the girl nevertheless retains her bubblegum. She even takes on a kind of individuality by becoming "the girl with the gum"; then, patterned after Smoker and Whistler, "the bubblegum girl."

The surprise came when I heard—again, a delayed reaction— a second meaning in the French for gum-chewer: *gommeuse*. A *gomme* can also mean "an eraser," or the one who erases, or in the case of this *gommeuse*, in other words, a personification of death.

(With that, I began to see the scene where my three little girls are driving the grumpy security guard crazy in a new light, and only then did I take in the full measure of what a coarsely macabre expression I was using to describe them in that scene: three little pests, as in *pestilence*.)

Constants, New Scenes, Variations

Once they are superimposed, and provided with backlighting, the three parchments of *The Secret of the Unicorn* allow the following message to be read:

> Three Brothers joyned. Three Unicorns in
> company sailing in the noonday Sunne will speak.
> For 'tis from the Light that Light will
> dawn. And then shines forth.
> 20 37 42N. 70 52 15W
> The Eagle's †

The text tells us nothing new: the words were already visible. It's the numbers that make all the difference in this final reading of the secret message, for they indicate the precise latitude and longitude of the treasure, whereas in the first version discovered by Tintin, this part of the message began with 42, then showed only a portion of the letter N, the digit 0 in 70, the 1 of 15, and only a portion of the W. Likewise, the numbers in the two succeeding versions were so incomplete that one could barely make out that they indicated degrees, minutes, or seconds, much less that the letters were meant to indicate compass points.

This is the model I adopted for my triptych, but with a few of my own variations:

1. I set myself the rule that each of my three sections—coconut palm, cargo ship, and centaur—would be self-contained. The story of Ti-Jus would be told start to finish, with all the pieces in place, each time.

2. Some scenes would be repeated in all three sections, others in only two of them, and still others would be unique. Modifying

or complementing one another, they would all be written into the same chronology. Still, from one section to another, the length of a scene might be dilated or condensed, just as narrative accelerations in the form of ellipses would not always occur at the same points in the story.

3. Whether a given scene is repeated or unique, in any case the text would be completely new each time out, since every section would be conceived after its own particular "fashion."

On the strength of these principles, I was able to draw up a kind of outline that laid out the various scenes of the novel, as well as setting up chronological schema that established over a period of about two weeks (day one + eleven or twelve days + final day) the concomitance or succession of these scenes. Not everything was set in stone—far from it. Many things only fell into place as I went along, not without a little fumbling. At least I was able to quickly decide on a scene breakdown that would apply to all three sections, one based essentially on the Book of Judith.

Constants

Three exposition chapters and a triggering event
In "The Coconut Palm" as in "The Cargo Ship" or "The Centaur," the first three chapters answer the classic questions Who, What, When, and Where.

Where and when? ... No longer in ancient Samaria, but today in Île-de-France, or the southern suburbs of Paris, to be precise. There's Bagneux, with its SUMABA, there's Ris-Orangis, with its Mermoz housing projects and its Vallon apartment complex, there's the suburban space between Bagneux and Ris-Orangis, with its highways and gridlock, Fresnes Prison, Thiais Cemetery . . .

Who? . . . First of all, Madame Fenerolo and Bessie Deux-Rivières, the first a supermarket manager, the second a cashier, seamstress, and mother. Ti-Jus, in keeping with the custom of the star making a tantalizingly late entrance, will appear only later, though the two women are already talking about him.

What? . . . What ordinarily takes place in a supermarket. Then, come closing time, and since the two women both live in Ris-Orangis, the manager gives the cashier a ride home through the dense rush-hour traffic. Their tête-à-tête serves as an occasion to hear Madame Fenerolo ask Bessie if she could do some alterations on a skirt of hers, and to learn that Bessie has already begun a different sewing job for her boss, a pantsuit. Here is where the triggering event occurs: a word, a gesture, an attitude on the part of Madame Fenerolo—nothing but a trifle, but a trifle tantamount to invasion, and sufficient to set destiny in motion, to spur the character fated to carry it out.

Two chapters that assess the violence of the four boys

In the next two chapters, Ti-Jus and his three buddies make their first appearance. In one way or another, this episode corresponds in each section with an irruption of violence that will foreshadow the final scene.

In "The Centaur," the four boys appear as early as the first chapter. But what is conveyed has more to do with their habits and life in the suburbs in general than with a particular scene, whereas what happens in chapters 4 and 5 follows the preestablished joint chronology of the book, and fulfills the same bridging function as their counterparts in the preceding sections.

Four chapters to follow up

What follows is the insidious expansion, in the landscape as well as in bodies and minds, of what was irreversibly unleashed by Madame Fenerolo's supposedly harmless statements or gestures in the car: a nameless, subjugating force that will soon plunge the inhabitants of the Mermoz Projects and of all Île-de-France into a state of consternation and give voice to their collective lamentations. What also follows is the completion of Bessie's tailoring job for Madame Fenerolo, after which Ti-Jus offers to deliver the goods for his mother, showers and dresses with care, and is finally on his way, switchblade in his pocket, accompanied by the hulk with the comb.

Two chapters for the denouement—or the problem of the severed head (and its resolution)

Final constant: in all three sections, the denouement is spread over two chapters. The garments are delivered, Madame Fenerolo goes alone to her bedroom to try them on, Ti-Jus joins her there . . . And we know how it ends, freely adapted from my Biblical model.

The severed head posed an awkward problem, nonetheless.

The decapitation scene constitutes the dramatic climax of the Book of Judith, a scene that a number of painters have chosen to depict. In the interest of combining grace with strength, and weight with suspension or elevation, these artists often show Holofernes's head already severed, a heavy load brandished briskly by a very feminine Judith . . . I wanted to preserve the decapitation. The question was how to avoid melodrama! . . .

My solution was as follows.

There would be no explicitly graphic decapitation, nor even any blood in the final scene. Though elsewhere in the novel blood would be in evidence, and in that way the severed head would manifest itself relentlessly.

This is why Ti-Jus showers and changes clothes before going over to Madame Fenerolo's, a kind of ritual cleansing prior to the sacrifice. He puts on a solar-yellow sweater, specially chosen, a pair of blue jeans specially slashed, as well as a leather jacket, "heartbreak red—color of spilt blood," whose texture had never appeared so animal, nor the color "so scarlet," to the astonishment of the hulk with the comb, in the centaur section.

As for the infamous head—though the reader is most probably unaware—it is severed well before the denouement and borne throughout the novel in all three sections, not by Ti-Jus himself, but by Celestin. In fact, I designed Ti-Jus's father to be a sort of precursor to his son, an aging alter ego, grown weary and practically annihilated either by some long incarceration (whence Bessie's distractedness when Madame Fenerolo's car drives them past Fresnes Prison), or by the weight of exile, hard labor, or trampled dignity . . .

Thus, in "The Coconut Palm," Celestin has a peculiar bearing, left shoulder raised, left arm slanted, left fist clenched tight, as though clutching, enraged, at some absent weight . . . (*HL* 1.06, p. 29)

And further on, he is compared to those

> ghosts reputed to return to the land of the living every evening at a fixed hour, in order to act out past crimes; or else to those ordinary individuals chosen by fate to commit some unspeakable act, in order to fulfill the destiny of the rest of the species, and who, burning with shame, take pity

on themselves at the very moment of their glory. (*HL* 1.06, p.30)

In "The Cargo Ship," when he goes down to buy a pack of loose tobacco at the Le Beuilhet Café, we see him collect his change "one-handed"—because the other is, in a sense, still bearing the eternal severed head—and the tobacconist at that moment

> keeps her eyes riveted to him, as though he is wounded, disfigured, monstrous, or has the absent look of figures in paintings carrying a dead body in their arms, or lifting a heavy decapitated head by the hair, and who, yoked to their load, seem themselves to have already entered the world beyond the grave, such that the living are stunned to discover them still in their midst. (*HL* 2.06, p. 80)

The head is not really there, and nowhere does the text make any explicit suggestion as to the nature of Celestin's past; but the idea that there is a certain similarity between the fates of father and son, and the image of Celestin carrying around the severed head—as if he were taking upon himself his son's future crime, or else had once committed the same crime himself—together determined every evocation of the character with all his traits and features, from his silence to his wobbly wandering about the apartment in the Mermoz Projects, not to mention the look in his eyes of a former boxer who has taken a few too many blows to the head.

But the severed head turns up elsewhere, too. It's what the title of the novel is referring to, the cry of the revenged as they watch their enemy's head roll off the scaffold—*Hoppla!*—as in the the Brechtian song which is quoted in my epigraph:

> *In that noonday heat there'll be a hush round the harbor*

As they ask which has got to die.
And you'll hear me as I softly answer: the lot!
And as the first head rolls I'll say: hoppla!

And then the head appears one more time, now in the final paragraph of "The Cargo Ship," where it is transformed into a bubblegum bubble blown by one of the Parcae-girls: the head of Holofernes, now Madame Fenerolo's head, is represented by this bubble in the remainder of the quotation I interrupted earlier, where the head is compared to an inflatable, head-sized ball:

> . . . her lips rounded to produce a huge chewing-gum bubble, making it look as though the girl had bent down in order to grab a toy balloon with her teeth. (*HL* 2.11, p. 106)

New Scenes

From coconut palm to cargo ship

Following the coconut-palm section, the cargo ship brings us new events, fresh material.

For instance, the dawn with its scene between the two truck drivers. Then the opening of the SUMABA, preceded by the gradual arrival of all its employees.

Likewise, in "The Cargo Ship," the appearance of Ti-Jus and his three buddies provides the occasion for a scene of vandalism, the only scene in the novel that actually takes place in Paris, and at the close of which, "running, all the while laughing, talking, panting," the four boys duck into the Gare de Lyon station "on the side where trains depart for the suburbs." Recall that in "The Coconut Palm," the same four boys were seen in just as big a hurry, laughing it up, talking nonstop, breathless, irrupting onto the platform where the Paris-Corbeil commuter train via Ris-Orangis was about to depart.

Other new additions: the love scene between Ti-Jus and the girl in the blue sweater, begun—but only just—in "The Coconut Palm"; or the long walk over to the Vallon Apartments by Ti-Jus and the hulk with the comb, and the welcome they receive from the three Parcae-girls.

From cargo ship to centaur

The centaur section also gives us some additional scenes.

The very first chapter presents Ti-Jus and his buddies brooding and bored in a room too small to hold them, prior to their long walk through the vast suburban wasteland.

Further on, the same quartet spends an evening at the Evry Bowling Alley. This establishment gets a mention in both the cargo and the coconut sections as well, but it's only in this third section that we learn it is a bowling alley in name only, and it's only in this section, in the space of a single chapter, that it becomes a theater of action—action that consists of a bloody brawl among the Mermoz boys and the gang called The Gardeners.

Likewise, it's only in "The Centaur" that a scene actually takes place inside the SUMABA; and finally, only in this section does the girl in the blue sweater come looking for Ti-Jus right where he lives.

Three times in *Hoppla!*, at the same sunset hour, the SUMABA closes its doors, and three times Madame Fenerolo and Bessie find themselves together in the manager's car, stuck in traffic. And thus, what I termed "the triggering event" earlier also takes place three times during their trip home.

But from one section to the next, the event itself changes.

In "The Coconut Palm," Madame Fenerolo is so annoyed by the stalled traffic that she "peremptorily presse[s] the OFF button" of her car radio. Earlier, in a perfectly calm voice, she shares an idea for a new project with her passenger:

"We might be opening a seafood department. That'd be nice, wouldn't it, a seafood department?" (*HL* 1.02, p. 10)

Finally, wanting to show Bessie what's wrong with the lining of the wraparound skirt she's wearing, she hikes up the garment while opening its flaps, without showing the slightest sign of embarrassment or unease, nor any feeling of feminine complicity or coquettishness . . .

> No, there was only a manager's gesture—exclusively and totally that, and thus the dazzlingly obvious fact that for Madame Fenerolo, there existed no possible mode of being aside from that of SUMABA manager. (*HL* 1.03, p. 14)

In "The Cargo Ship," we find the same situation, and the same move, on the part of the driver, to switch off the radio, the same allusion to the future installation of a seafood department at the SUMABA.

> "It'll be nice, don't you think, Bessie, a seafood counter?" (*HL* 2.03, p. 68)

But the text now tells us how the answer to this pseudo-question is forced upon Bessie, the acquiescence already present in the words that make up the question, present consequently in the mouth of the manager, then released into the cabin of the car, where, "convinced it's right," it prowls, "calmly committing its violence."

Same situation in "The Centaur." This time, the seafood department gets mentioned earlier: between two ads, the loudspeakers that deliver regular messages to the SUMABA shoppers announce that the new department will soon be opening. But, apart from this, there is the same traffic jam on the way to Ris-Orangis, the same chilly rain, and, in the car, the same soothing voice coming over the car radio—until the moment when "in a fit of rage" the manager hits the button and shuts off the radio. The text adds: "and this made all the difference." Then:

> Switching off a car radio was a harmless gesture. A show of temper in such circumstances was perfectly understandable. Thus, the *THIS* in *this made all the difference* pertains not to the gesture itself, nor even to the acerbic abruptness of its execution, but to the fact that the manager had so fully and unreservedly embodied the meanness and viciousness of her gesture. (HL 3.03, p. 120)

There are numerous episodes that, like these three versions of the same key moment, undergo transformations throughout my novel, each fully developed in its own way.

This is the case with scenes directly derived from the Book of Judith: invasion, lamentation, preparations, descent into the valley/Vallon, the final face-to-face encounter. This is also the case with other scenes whose origins are not so ancient: Madame Fenerolo and Bessie in the car together, stuck in traffic on the Île-de-France highway system; Madame Fenerolo at Bessie's place for a fitting; or Ti-Jus and the girl in the blue sweater making love in an apartment they have broken into for the occasion.

But inside this or that scene, there are also units made up of only a few lines or a few words that from one section to the next revitalize the presentation of the same micro-event. I hope, through the example I'm about to give, to highlight the way certain of these variations were directly and wholly determined by my three title motifs.

Here it is.

Ti-Jus and the hulk with the comb are at Madame Fenerolo's. The package they have just delivered has been set on the living-room table. First, dubious behavior occurs, then tension starts to mount . . . This is the situation in all the sections. At this juncture, however, things diverge. In "The Coconut Palm," we have:

> Outside, a car was slowly maneuvering between the front and rear buildings. Its tires were making a continuous unsticking sound on the asphalt, or else a dull crackling on the fine gravel; a sound, in either case, that could in no way compare with the silky, heartrending rasp that such tires would have produced on sand . . . (*HL* 1.10, p. 48)

But in "The Cargo Ship":

> Outdoors, a car was maneuvering between the two buildings of the apartment complex in first gear, its tires on the asphalt making a continuous unsticking noise, a mellow lapping, periodically swelling to more of a short, low sucking sound. (*HL* 2.11, p. 102)

Finally, in "The Centaur":

And when, in a little while, rising from below, a lapping
sound is heard, that of four tires moving in first gear, even
this sound, however familiar, conjures up not so much the
visitors' parking lot as those silted terrains where the leg
sinks knee-deep: the shallows of some backwater, a path
forged by a relentless procession, soaked by a monsoon; or
the endlessly trampled shores of a river where zebra, buf-
falo, and other animals gather to quench their thirst in the
brown water at set times. (*HL* 3.11, p. 158)

The sound of tires is evoked each time, leading us into the words
describing them, words which, while taking us somewhat outside
the tightly enclosed area where the action is taking place, also conjure up a space entirely incongruous and foreign to the story: that of
an endless line of coconut palms along a sandy shore; that of a harbor where water laps nonchalantly against the hull of a docked ship;
and again, that of a landscape marked by the prints of wild animals,
in the calm before the storm, a tropical tornado in fact, the centaurlike outburst of my suburban hero.

Open it up, give it some room to breathe! . . . I felt a consistent need
to do so throughout the writing of *Hoppla! 1 2 3*. I felt that a peri-
odic expansion of the landscape would give the story some breathing room, while in terms of the narrative action, such an opening
up could convert the tension associated with an expectation, a fear,
a hitch, or a resentment into something more dynamic.

But enlarging the setting wasn't enough. I also had to poke a few
holes in the fiction to allow these sudden incursions into the story
from far outside the confines of its narrative frame, giving rise to a

sense of depth, the sense of an elsewhere, of unlimited possibilities within the text itself . . . It was a way of saving the story from sinking into the kind of sordidness typical, no doubt, of our own, *real* stories. Whatever the case, my ambition was to breathe some life into this story, to raise it to a certain altitude . . . Call it "the sublime," if you will—from the Latin *sublimis*, "raised high." "The echo of a great soul," says Longinus. And among the various examples he puts forth in his famous treatise,[8] he cites the silence of Ajax . . . This has to do with an episode told in chapter XI of the *Odyssey*, during which Odysseus, on the threshold of Hades, addresses the shades of his former companions. Set apart from the others is the shade of Ajax,[9] whom Odysseus notices and attempts to cajole. But Ajax turns away and, without a word, slinks back into the shadowy gloom.

Taking inspiration from this prestigious model, and since Ti-Jus already wasn't exactly talkative even in my first draft of *Hoppla!*, I considered including a scene where my protagonist's sublime silence would elevate the text to Homeric heights . . . I imagined the scene's opening, development, and climax. All I needed was to find a suitable place in *Hoppla!*'s succession of chapters and events, and then write it . . . But, alas! I couldn't seem to fit it anywhere, there weren't any opportunities to get it started. So that even though Ti-Jus remained the silent type from start to finish, the grand scene, the

---

8 Longinus, *On the Sublime*. In his preface to the Rivages Poche edition, Jackie Pigeaud specifies that the sublime "requires strength and even violence, youth and agility . . ." all qualities that I take pleasure in ascribing to Ti-Jus.

9 Having been unable to obtain the weapons of Achilles, attributed to Odysseus, Ajax took his own life.

summation of his silence was not to take place. And I, the author, was left with the tentative hope that my aborted plan would not all be for naught, that the unembodied sublimity of my project had somehow been conserved as a memory, a spirit, or a shadow, nested within the thickness of the printed characters on the page or haunting the blank spaces between lines.

ANECDOTES

ANECDOTE: odd little fact whose telling can bring
to light a hidden reality. —*Le Robert* dictionary

Oil Palms and Coconut Palms

Wedged between laguna and ocean, the road leading out of Cotonou runs twenty kilometers up to Sémé-Kpodji; then, after an interminable bend that leaves nearby Nigeria on the right, it pulls away from the coastline, tracking north another ten kilometers before reaching a narrow bridge that marks the entrance into Porto-Novo.

But whenever I make the trip, as I often do, I feel I'm driving on a thin, asphalted cordon that separates oil palms from coconut palms.

The oil palm side is dull, dark, aridly earthy, full of rough uneven spots. The air is stuffy and a musty, muddy smell rises from the wells. As if that wasn't enough, everything there seems to have long since given way to disorder and folly.

Is it because the coconut-palm side is exactly the opposite? Or does my fondness for coconuts come from a primordial familiarity?
. . .
Whatever the reason, I feel I belong to the coconut side.

Rapture with Babar and Mallarmé

The first picture shows a bourgeois drawing room circa Third Republic France, with carpet on a chevron-patterned parquet, Louis XV armchairs, gold-framed mirror over the fireplace . . . Babar is leaning on the mantelpiece. Fashionably dressed to suit the décor, with his spats and wing collar, the young elephant tells a rapt audience of his childhood in the great forest.

In another picture, Mallarmé receives visitors, just as he would do every Tuesday in his Paris apartment on the Rue de Rome. Here it is he the guests are listening to, it is he who leans against the mantelpiece.

And today, I in turn play the same role of worldly storyteller—in the *salon* of another era, with fireplace and listeners all included.

A lady reacts to my first story: "At the age of four? That young?" Then her surly neighbor: "Impossible!"—before adding, suddenly all sweetness, that my little story was charming nonetheless.

The story in question is a childhood memory dating back to my first year in Anse Vata—so I really was only four. Hina and I never hung out together much. We didn't share the same desk or the same bench in Madame S's class, nor did we play or chat together on the playground, or see one other in the city. And yet it was Hina, and no other, who repeatedly featured upon the stage of my fantasies all that year: I would lift her up, effortlessly, and, airborne myself, carry her away; she was sweet and lovely, as I would see her every week, five days out of seven, naked, as I never saw her in real life; our synchronized flight would last and last, secure, tender, simple, delightful.

The incredulous listener shakes his head.
"An illusion," he insists. "A mnemonic mirage, classic!"
I let him have his say, sure of my memory.

A Cargo Ship's Wake

From the gangway, Moussa had just sent him a discrete signal, so that the commanding officer rose and, changing for just an instant the good-natured atmosphere that prevailed in the mess, a bit solemn despite his open shirt and jeans, he spread his arms.

"Gentlemen . . ."

We sat down to dinner.

The table was set for eight, with one setting untouched until the second-in-command went to relieve the lieutenant on the bridge. Moussa was complimented on his white jacket and entrusted with the mission to congratulate the cook on his lamb stew. Conversation turned once again to the previous night's incident. A sluice valve had been turned in the wrong direction, which triggered flooding in the machine room and set off an alarm. Even the officer in training smiled at his blunder.

Our stories went further back in time.

Various boats were evoked, various points on the globe, some funny occurrence, some peril or loss connected with each ship and each location. For instance, one stormy day off the coast of Barbados, Youenn the chief mechanic thought that the *Baie-des-Anges* was capsizing. *Baie-des-Anges* was the twin craft of the *Cap Canaille*, both roll-on roll-off ships built according to the same specs at the same shipyard at Saint-Nazaire. Yet there were never two boats more unlike than these. *Baie-des-Anges* was faulty in every way—prone to listing, shuddering, hard to maneuver—whereas the other . . . Youenne had sailed everywhere on the *Cap Canaille*. So there was the story about the crazy guy in a pedal boat in the middle of the

North Sea, or the boat people in the Java Sea, or that group binge in Pointe-à-Pitre, and all the lay days that had cost the ship owner a fortune . . .

The second-in-command slipped away and soon the lieutenant joined our table. When the meal was over, we dispersed. Again, a sharp hammering rose from the hold, accompanied by the humming of the engines. Still, these noises didn't keep me from noting the stillness of the surrounding gangways or of that even vaster silence farther on, almost sidereal in span, into which the *Cap Canaille* was heading, as it rocked ever so slightly. I went on deck to get some air, ascended to the upper bridge, and from there climbed up to the poop deck, without meeting a soul. The sun was beating down hard. The only cloud in the Mediterranean sky was the smoke of the cargo ship stretching its long cumulus behind the stern, and equally isolated on the water's flat surface, our wake was tracing a lifeline whose constant erasure in the distance revived all possibilities, made all directions, all destinations perfectly conceivable.

Even the traffic noise from the nearby highway and the roar of planes taking off from Orly Airport were drowned out by the shrill rasping of the buzz saw. Rather than trying to scream over the noise so that Raf and I could hear him, the ironworker pointed wordlessly to a line-up of old car doors; looking skeptical, he seemed to be saying, go ahead, but you won't find it.

We looked, but didn't find.

Raf shouted the suggestion that maybe at Rosny, at that Croatian's place . . .

We got back on the road—the A6, soon the A86, with their four lanes in either direction. Raf was grumbling, clearly annoyed that Amadou, when lending us his car, hadn't agreed to reinstall the radio. He went on to say that he knew these parts, including in *these parts* not only the department of Essonne, but the entire area of zones 94 and 93. Then something about traffic jams, about the other day, about a girlfriend of his. And when he called someone on his cell, he suddenly looked more alive while his eyes seemed to wander into the distance; he would start the conversation with a jovial "Raf here," before indicating who he was with and toward which Île-de-France destination we were heading.

In Rosny, having as little success as we'd had in Chilly-Mazarin, we agree we've had enough of junkyards for one day. All right, so what do we do now? Where to? Raf has several friends in Livry-Gargan. He also knows a girl in Bondy, who he was going to call to let her know that—well, maybe not, it's getting late by now, and so I drop off Raf and the car in Chelles, at Amadou's.

On foot now, and alone in the waning light, I make my way to the RER station at Noisy-Champs. Walking beside the strip malls, the housing projects, the wait on the platform, the trip, changing trains at Châtelet-Les Halles . . . It's going to take me hours!

And yet, I feel relieved.

It's just that I can't stand the place where Amadou lives. It reeks of old age, of housebound boredom, of death. Here at least there are no little houses with their little gardens; space here has scope, and the highways perched on their concrete pylons look positively eminent in the landscape.

Metro

Each in charge of a fifth grade class at the *Ecole urbaine* in Porto-Novo, the schoolmasters Kovi and d'Almeïda are dismayed: on this exam-day morning, an unsolvable math problem involving the rate of flow of a quantity of hot water, then the dictation assignment read by someone with dreadful pronunciation, and now this *canari*[10] business in the précis topic!

For the last item on the test, the first major exam of the term, their students have all been told to write a précis of a story read to them, one entitled "The Elephant and the Canary," which has been or will have been read aloud, depending on one's longitudinal location on the globe, to all test-takers in France and French possessions overseas. They find the text, which contains dialogue between its two eponymous creatures, strange: that an elephant might speak, fine—the animal has a mouth, after all, is intelligent, a mammal, a distant cousin to man, even, somehow—but a *canari*!

Most of the assignments written in Porto-Novo will get respectable enough grades, in the end, even though, without exception, these pupils imagined this *canari* not as a bird but as one of those clay pots that housewives or their daughters balanced on their heads.

The same relativity exists for the word *metro*.

As long as I was living in Anse Vata, and then when I moved to the boulevard on the laguna, the word evoked not so much an urban

---

10   Translator's note: The French word *canari* translates as "canary" in English, but in Creole French, it also refers to a clay pot.

mass-transit system as a particular currency—the "metro franc" in use prior to the euro, called the "CPF franc" in the Pacific Ocean territories and the "CFA franc" in French West Africa—or as another word for *zoreille*,[11] which we shortened to "zozo" . . . thus, "metro," for me will always be a term designating someone living in the far-flung territories, but hailing from the distant and ambivalent French motherland.

---

11   Creole term from French *les oreilles* (ears), to designate White Europeans in the colonies and overseas possessions. Several explanations: Europeans strain their ears to understand local Creole, or their ears turn bright red in the tropical sun, etc.

THE ORINOCO

She served me my drink first, before my female companions at the table, then explained why: the serving order wasn't not a sign of impoliteness to the ladies, but of her own weakness for men.

Yet, something about her smile, her voice, the way she moved, deepened my sense that I had already met this woman . . . Indeed, even her establishment had immediately felt familiar, though I had never been there before. I had often noticed the sign, had more than once promised to have a meal there, but until today, I'd never actually done so—no more than I'd ever traveled to or even made a stopover in French Guiana, nor, consequently, ever seen the Orinoco, the river after which the restaurant was named. Parisian restaurant, Guianese river, if I somehow feel a strange affinity for both, it must be that the broad brown flow of water or the primeval forest, and certain peppery flavors, certain clouds of mosquitoes, certain ex-convicts returned from the penal colony, and numerous other accumulated memories, were revived all at once when the restaurant owner stood over me, while behind her I saw a large picture on the wall depicting a panoramic view of a canoe heading down the Orinoco.

The Painting of the Queen

In the midst of embossed wallpaper, patterned carpet, and translucent windows, the beer drinkers in London pubs talk passionately of cricket, Xmas, Eurostar, tube accidents. While I, at the Warren Street Station, coming up the multilevel escalator that conveys travelers to the surface, see—instead of the customary advertising posters—a sloping parade of a single, repeated ad, announcing a temporary exhibit at the National Gallery: "The Queen's Pictures." The poster displays a reproduction of *Judith*, or at least one of the *Judith*s, by Cristofano Allori, a painting whose image, incessantly encountered in this late December, will come to decorate my office, in postcard format, throughout the six long years it will take me to write *Hoppla! 1 2 3*.

Nothing but the butchered head here, no blood—except if one includes the richly scarlet lining of Judith the butcher's cloak. But even more than by Allori's softening/sublimation of the scene, I am struck by his ambiguous, if not perverse, depiction of the heroine. From her pale cheeks, ever so slightly rosy, her heavy eyelids, and her extended neck, emphasizing her strained position, there emerges a feeling of sorrow and fragility. Yet, at the same time, her body speaks pointedly of vigor and steadfastness, even a fierceness of spirit, in both the stability of her pose and the rigid tension of her outstretched arm bearing its sword, and even more, in the tensed fist that, in the foreground, joints white with strain, holds up by a thick tuft of hair its gory trophy.

I'm surprised today at having begun even then to set aside documents and notes in a special *Judith* file. *Hoppla!* hadn't yet come into being at that time, not even as an idea . . . But in this unconscious anticipation, I want to see a sign—a sign that this story has always had me in mind; that for a long time now, in any case, its heroine has been watching me, hovering.

Coconut Crabs

For a few weeks more, the port development project not yet having commenced, the sand still stretches uninterrupted along several kilometers between the old wooden wharf and the aerodrome, so that it's only a short distance to cover whenever we feel like having a swim. From the deserted spot where we've just set down our towels and removed our flip-flops, we need only turn our heads to catch sight of the house, or if not the house, then at least the row of *filao* trees that buffer it from the seafront road, as well as the flag raised every morning on the pole of our terrace, flying the very recently proclaimed national colors.

Véronique—she will confide this much later—is scared out of her wits by this place; not because of the size and thunderous roar of the waves, nor the brutal suction of the undertow, but because of the plethora of coconut crabs in the immediate vicinity. By the hundreds, perhaps thousands, during the brief interval between two crashing waves, these crabs leave their holes as if to stretch their legs and explore a bit—half bold, half anxious—scurrying over both wet sand and dry . . . As for myself, back on the Sémé beach where they also used to swarm, I would play at hunting them or just watch them for hours as they went about their business . . . These coconut crabs are tiny transparent crustaceans, so light as to be nearly immaterial, harmless even to the skin of a three-year-old girl. Still, the sight of their teeming numbers all around us used to terrorize my little niece.

A Story to Come

We were just pulling in as another boat was pulling out, one whose name we could only make out with our telescope, *The Iolaos*. "*The Iolaos!*" exclaimed Jean-Pierre, "that's Luc's boat, isn't it?" The two friends had just missed each other. Then, while the pilot was coming on board, I went ahead a bit, leaving Jean-Pierre to greet him, and leaned on the railing of the promenade deck to watch the approach of land. Already, after a long while as nothing more than a cone seeming to emerge out of flat water, the island now looked like a portion of continent, just as, conversely, the city would soon be reduced to a harbor area as we pulled away from land, though for the moment it was still displayed in all its panoramic horizontality, offering its full scope to my view.

And now, we are moored along the B2 dock, stern to prow with a cargo ship that must have docked just before we did. A crane is busy at work starboard while recently disembarked passengers seek information from the port authorities or seamen, negotiate with porters, drivers, or begin dispersing. Among them, I notice a man wearing a Panama hat who seems the very embodiment of freshness, of brisk cologne—a freshness that would resist the ambient heat, a cologne with a discreet but bracing scent, that would remain unaltered by the strong mingling odors of iodine, copra, and fuel-soaked sawdust. He's with another man, who looks like he's a native. Or at least, as he points at crates stacked up on a trolley, waves to a far-off acquaintance in the midst of all the land-based excitement and commotion, or else points out the port authority building—under construction—to his companion, he's acting like someone who knows his way around . . . I assume the new arrival is moving here for two or three years. For the first few days, everything will astonish him. Then he'll get used to it all, settle into his habits, start to identify the country with the few places he'll get to know, even identify with the country himself. Finally, torn between pleasure and regret, he'll watch his departure date approach. He will have experienced an entire story . . . For an instant, I envy him. And when the white Panama hat has disappeared from view, I am overcome with melancholy . . . The feeling quickly dissolves, however, for at the last minute I catch an exchange of glances between the man in the hat and a lady—they had been hastily introduced; she seemed in a rush, but after a few steps in the direction of the docked ships, she stopped and looks back, at the same time the man in the hat is turning back toward her.

Stallion with Young Boy on the Banks of the Niger

To the north, without transition, is the desert, where nothing grows but a few prickly plants, and where on certain days, nomad camps appear in the trembling light of an intense heat wave.

To the south, the city is likewise brought to an abrupt halt by the river, beyond which the dry, flat stretches of the savanna are preceded only by a narrow band of greenery. On the bridge joining the two riverbanks, there is almost no traffic. Except when military maneuvers are taking place, and not counting people on foot, one is likely to see more bicycles and scooters than four-wheel vehicles. One might occasionally see a horseman riding across, or a camel driver whose rich robes billow in the wind; or a donkey driver goading his beast of burden; or even one of those animal herds where zebus and goats mingle, tended by tall, ascetic-looking shepherds. Though most of the time, these herders prefer to ford the river a few hundred meters upstream, so as to touch ground in the city at Baobab Strand.

This is where I will see the little boy.

Part meadow, part vacant lot, Baobab Strand occupies a large undeveloped space between the river and the boulevard. I hardly ever stop there, even though we pass by in our pick-up truck every afternoon, and the place has always held a certain attraction for me. No herd today, not even any of the large canoes that sometimes disembark passengers with their bundles. Nothing out of the ordinary: a sparse population, activity slow paced, made up of disjointed mini-scenes whose actors resemble tiny figurines.

The stallion in the midst of all this is motionless, massive enough to give an impression of weightlessness to the boy riding astride his spine. The boy seems in no hurry to make the animal move, nor is he moving himself, absorbed as he is in watching the river flow by. Even before anything happens, I am struck by this shared immobility of horse and boy; perhaps also, with one the harnessed by only a rope and the other dressed in mere underpants, by their shared nudity. Then all of a sudden, the horse's penis slips out of its sheath and stretches calmly to the ground.

The landscape suddenly evacuates all material presence. As a background to the murmur softly rising from Baobab Strand, nothing but a stream of silence attests that the river is still there; as for the two or three washerwomen and their multicolored basins, the handyman cyclist with his assortment of monkey wrenches, the group of men in conversation, or the little girl with a baby on her back, all these, and the remainder of the visible world have disappeared as though in an excess of light, save the stallion with a hard-on and the little boy.

Not a drop of rain has fallen for three months, yet the humidity level is such that packaged food, clothing, the passengers' bodies, and various other items in the car all spontaneously express their odors. Mingled with the after-smells of mold and rust, this peculiar composite scent makes up a substantial part of our shared taxi's identity.

The atmosphere is otherwise lively, with hilarity occasionally getting the better of controversy, and the storytellers' vehement facial contortions always dramatizing their tales. Thus, it is only when we catch up with the train that left Porto-Novo before we did that our attention is finally diverted to the outside world. In addition to the railroad tracks, there are oil palm trees are out there, scattered among the underbrush and the few scrubby farmed plots. Here and there are also the cinder blocks of an abandoned construction site or the corrugated metal of some roof, and the usual reddish brown earth of a termite mound, a wall, a path, all perfectly ordinary, like some immutable backdrop, the only distinctive feature of the season being the absence of puddles, now long since dried up, and an overabundance of dust, which now more than ever deadens even the most rugged evergreens.

At about kilometer eleven, centrifugal force begins to make our upper bodies lean in unison. Usually, as we come out of a bend, we see ahead of us the long straight line of road growing ever narrower as it stretches toward the vanishing point. But today, surprise! Less than half a kilometer ahead, an opaque wall between land and sky blocks all perspective, a motionless mass getting shinier and louder the closer we get. Then, all of a sudden, we've entered a downpour.

The passengers are bubbling over—cries, fidgeting, laughter. The din of rain pelting the windshield and hood, instantly inundated.

The shower's strength lies undoubtedly in its suddenness. All the more in that we drove right into it, rather than its coming to us.

But there is something else.

From now on, it's going to rain every day. It's late March, and the rainy season will last until mid-July. At the moment of our irrupting into the rain, I thus became conscious not only of entering a new space, but of changing seasons, just as when we step over a threshold we sometimes feel we've somehow entered the future—it is here we will be living henceforth, within these walls, among these objects, seeing this landscape, all unfamiliar to our past life—or when on a ship passing the dateline we marvel at tipping into an hour we have already experienced, and that we will just this once relive.

After the Hurricane

Though Grande Terre didn't get hit as hard as the islands, the hurricane did tear off a corner of our metal roof, rip several window screens, and shift the back of the house by about twenty centimeters. Worried perhaps by the intermittent whistling caused by some last winds, or simply glad for a well-earned respite after the turmoil, people are reluctant to leave their homes. So, as we drive toward the Orphelinat district, we hardly encounter a single vehicle, apart from the garbage collectors. The sidewalks are still strewn with trash and debris. Here and there the road is cluttered with tree branches, packing cartons, a TV antenna: an obstacle course we must steer through with care.

And what about the coconut palms?

Most of them are untouched, bearing not even a trace of last night's turmoil. Several, however, have been so roughed up that they are now oddly disheveled, or worse, headless, bereft of all foliage, reduced to the wretchedness of a skinny, bare trunk. I can't resist singling out these specimens. And, years later, I see them still, just as I see the coconut palms along the corniche leaning over the laguna, and the coconut palms rising above the mangrove, and those rooted into the mountainside reaching their fronds into the void . . . From these, I learned with each passing day how light dances, seeing them sway, filtering the sun, then letting it surge through. The sight of the others, however, the day after the hurricane, provided me with a blunt initiation to disaster.

A Square Somewhere in the Hauts-de-Seine

I get off the train at an hour when the exits from the RER station allow for passage right onto the Rue des Blagis, which leads directly to where I live. So hardly am I off the commuter train from Paris when I'm walking down the middle of a narrow street, void of any vehicles, apart from those parked along the sidewalks. The neighborhood is perfectly silent. The little houses themselves and their gardens seem to slumber behind their fences, enclosures, hedges of rushes, the din of invisible traffic reaching my ears as though from some other world off in the distance. In such a setting, once again I have a keen sense of my own existence, and consequently that of all the many places I carry around with me ever since I lived in each. I refer to them by type of domicile: the Orphelinat house, the makeshift dwelling at Anse Vata, the *Sagittaire* cargo ship, the apartment building on Rue de la Ferme near the Seine, the house on the laguna boulevard, the house on the seafront boulevard, the Villa Bamboo, near the port, the desert view house, etc.

Then, as I reach the big intersection, Carrefour de la Libération, I am suddenly walking into noisy, open space in which all sorts of other spaces emerge. Neighborhoods, commons, localities in this area; but there are also places more distant that are nonetheless co-extensive with where I am, and with those places most integral to my being. Not these earthbound places, but rather those that float, as if weightless, forever shifting in an aerial continuum, sometimes moving apart, sometimes coming together, combining for just an instant—and in so doing, recalling that old Perrier ad: in a bar, people and objects represented on posters come to life; then, leaving the confines of their frames, taking on a third dimension, they mingle with real people and objects in the bar to partake in a hectic, totally improbable dance number . . . Bar customers and racehorses, a waiter, a diva, a glass of Perrier, and a tennis champion glide by within the same space, rubbing shoulders, layered one upon the other though never colliding.

THE SLEEP ATTACK

It's pouring rain, on this last day of the rainy season, and having completed an errand that didn't actually take that long, I arrive soaking wet in front of the cathedral where Paulin was supposed to wait for me in the Peugeot 504. But there's neither a 504 nor Paulin anywhere to be seen. To check whether the driver might not have sought shelter in the cathedral, and to get out of the rain myself, I enter the nave. Five or six of the supplicant faithful are scattered about in the half-light, as well as a few sleepers stretched out here and there on a pew.

Later, Paulin tells me he was one of the sleepers—and to explain why: THE COOL AIR GRABBED ME AND I WAS ATTACKED BY SLEEP.

Words like these, arranged and pronounced with just enough conviction, help reenact the ambush such that we relive the moment of assault, the treacherous alacrity of the two aggressors as they pounce. They render honorable, or at least understandable, the swift capitulation of the victim. They also demonstrate what language stands to gain by being slightly disturbed, in both senses of the word: its usual order disrupted and likewise tinged with madness.

An analogous oddity: *Hotel Franklin and of Brazil*. I never knew the hotel thus named, which, according to old Parisian phonebooks, was located at 19 Rue Buffault, near the Cadet metro station. On the other hand, not far from the Luxembourg Gardens, there was once another hotel I used to pass by, whose name jostles syntax in the same manner. It was called *Hotel* (a proper noun with no article or preposition) *and the United Provinces*, or *United Principalities*, I don't recall which. My research in the Archives of the City of Paris proved fruitless, and various inhabitants of the quarter that I questioned have no recollection of a hotel with a name of that sort. The only trace attesting that this strange sign ever did exist resides in the double appellation I assigned to a fictitious Parisian *pension* in one of my novels, in imitation of this now lost model—the lodgings of a certain Explorer who ventures at once into the labyrinth of streets, the jungle of meaning, and the deciphering of signs: *Hotel Nessus and of Café Mimile.*

CHOOSING ACHILLES

For a long time, I preferred Hector to Achilles, since Achilles seemed to muddle all sorts of well-established categories: man, woman, heroism, virtue . . . I reproached him for subjugating bravery to mood; for his lack of self-possession; for being too sensitive and graceful, like a girl, thereby allowing femininity to seep into the core of virility.

Later on, he was to become one of my favorite heroes.

I was moved as much by the nervous collapses suffered by this temperamental, magnificent figure as by his outbursts of anger. I loved all the stories about him. Whether in the temple or the gyneceum, at sea, in his tent, on the battlefield, swift to flee the Amazon Penthesilia and then ferocious when laying her low, only to be seized by an exalted love, I found this character sublime. But what enthralled me most was imagining his education, being put through his paces under the expert guidance of Chiron the centaur, learning to play the lyre, practicing swordsmanship, even mounting his mentor and prancing about, or swimming alongside him when learning his strokes.

Whence this change of heart?

I have no idea. All I do know is that one day, I chose Achilles; that one day it was finally possible for me to choose Achilles, or not even choose, but concede that unbeknownst to me, this choice within me had taken place, and that I was pleased with it.

It seems to me that where my personal penchants are concerned, another evolution is currently taking place, one that will culminate in my growing affinity for oil palms, ousting my current favorite, the coconut.

Does that mean I'll have to distance myself from the coconut palm? Will this be a gradual blinding or an epiphany? Maturity, aging, denial or what . . . ?

THE PANAMA CANAL

On the world map, the blue of the oceans drowned the islands or subsumed them into the nearest continent, alternating land and sea in a few large, contrasting masses. Hence, the Americas found themselves wedged between two worlds, separating them better than any wall, better than a series of mountain chains placed end to end. I was coming from the west. The names that flecked the Pacific, though hardly designating territories of substance, signified for me a friendly, brotherly terrain. The Atlantic world, on the other hand, remained foreign, distant in my worldview, even though I was born on its shores, as we drew closer and closer to Panama.

Was it going to feel like entering a new life, going through the canal?

Not at all. When the time arrived, novelty came in the shape of the same old sea and swell, and the same old sky beneath which our journey resumed its familiar course. The canal was nothing but a parenthesis, and it was then that I felt, more than ever before, that all the places I've traveled are contiguous in my mind, points definitively lined up to trace the journey of a life whose next stops will be called Curaçao, Las Palmas, Marseille, just as the most recent were Papeete, Suva, Anse Vata, or the Orphelinat quarter.

In the meantime, incongruously flanked by land and cattle, our cargo ship, as though a freshwater boat, was towed along two cement docks. It then passed through the series of locks, gradually changing altitude. I found the situation entertaining, though somehow embarrassing at the same time—we resembled those circus elephants one sometimes sees in transport, lifted into the air and slowly pivoting at the end of a sling, just some trivial airborne bundle.

An Encounter in the Sands

I'm sitting on the stoop of my house looking out onto the desert when I hear, coming from behind the house, a woman's voice singing in Tahitian. To recognize instantly the strains of the *Manu e* from my Pacific years, and what's more, to suspect the voice singing it to be the same as the one that first introduced the song to me, all this fills me suddenly with nostalgia—but for which period, in fact? Which country . . . ?

Less a specific period, to tell the truth, than the whole of my past; and less a specific country than all the places that have invited me in, in succession or alternation, today decked out in their shiniest brass, their warmest waters, their sunniest coconut palms, their reddest laterite against the background of forest or savannah, as well as their finest metro system, their tallest glass-and-steel towers—but decked out for what purpose?

To welcome within myself the city where I am now living among houses, donkeys, and camels, all the same earthen color, looking out on the sands that stretch out to the horizon.

Yester-places, that the song brought back intact, and today's place where the song has caught up with me, the Tahitian tune brings them together, condensing into a single event everything experienced in both the past and present places, be these dreams, expectations, or adventures, in the same way that, in a first meeting, two lives suddenly stream together, each having heretofore borne its own story alone: Solomon and the Queen of Sheba; Kurtz and Marlow, in *Heart of Darkness*; or Diogenes and Alexander—"Stand a little out of my sun"; or Stanley and Livingstone—"Dr. Livingstone, I presume."

The climb was getting increasingly difficult for the old Citroën 2CV. Was it going to break down? And if it did, how would I press on, and avoid having to go back to Allada?

I had just spent two miserable days there, and the sound of drums that had kept me up all night was still pounding in my head. Moreover, I still felt a certain unease over my encounter with the ghost. In his traditional colorful dress, bells on his heels, face mask of painted wood, he was escorted by a troupe of kids who, without showing any overt fear of him, did nevertheless keep a cautious distance. I had come across these ghost figures several times already in the streets of Porto-Novo. They had never paid any attention to me, whereas this one today had turned toward me when he arrived at where I was standing. For an instant, before a change of heart, he had even seemed on the verge of approaching me. His young escorts all stopped and watched me for a long while, as if, one might have thought, to commit my facial features to memory.

Everything changes a kilometer later. The landscape is still low scrub forest, relieved here and there by pale grass, ferruginous earth, or black patches caused by slash-and-burn. But then, its slim trunk rising above its surroundings, the only specimen of its kind in this zone, deploying its fronds far above the cola trees and wild mangoes, a coconut palm has appeared, a scout come to soothe the survivor . . . With that, the motor of the 2CV suddenly seems to be working better, the slope seems less steep, the blacktop less gooey below the tires. Euphoric just to be back on flat road, I'm soon chanting to myself: made it! made it!

DOUBLE PONIES

P has also noticed the building in question, with its stable stall doors and a bronze horse head in the middle of the façade, along which is inscribed HORSE TRADERS, PONIES, DOUBLE PONIES, PONIES OF ALL ORIGINS, DRAFT HORSES. We pronounce HORSE TRADERS together, and then, laughing, read the rest out loud with delight. Then P asks me what "double pony" means.

The nonsensical English-language term "double pony" designates, in French, an intermediary size between pony and horse, suitable for younger riders. This is something I think I know, and am thus ready to give my answer to the question. But I realize at this very instant that the answer has somehow escaped me. In a panic, I search madly through my memory, alarmed to find nothing under the heading "double pony."

This particular experience reminds me of the one we've all known, living in a country where we don't speak the language. Yet, if the particular circumstances of the pony problem turned this sensation into an ordeal, I generally find the memory of my times as a foreigner to be a pleasant one. For although I have been through this experience many times, I've never been left with the impression of being an outsider, outside the language: on the contrary, I was always able to savor the theatricality of speech from the privileged position of both free actor and crude witness. Free actor in that I would conduct monologues with myself with a feeling of heightened impunity. And crude witness in that, unburdened as I was by any concern for understanding the words, I could hear in the expression of voices the prodigal expenditure of life breath and of energy, while at the same time seeing how involved the speakers would become, how contorted their faces, how physically animated. In short, I would discover how much, under cover of meaning, language makes us mad.

Knowing that, at the Jaurès Café, "coffee" by itself stands for coffee spiked with calvados, I've ordered a "café without calva." There are a dozen of us regulars lined up along the counter, with only two or three tables occupied in the rest of the café. Outside, a group of pedestrians on their way home from the nearby RER train station disperse hastily into the pre-dawn gloom. Traffic is heavy. It seems to stretch to infinity, producing a noise ill-suited to the quiet back streets of the city center.

Then something happens.

Having foolishly entered a limited-clearance underpass that tunnels beneath the train lines, a driver has got his truck stuck. Soon, gaping onlookers have gathered around. I join them . . . The top of the truck is rubbing right up against the smooth concrete ceiling of the underpass, and the driver is nowhere to be seen. He's probably gone to seek help; or perhaps, in a panic, he's simply fled the scene—in any case his vehicle is empty, abandoned to the eyes and excited commentary of the curious bystanders.

But a man's voice suddenly takes us to task, a strong, hoarse voice. The man is visibly inebriated, delirious perhaps. With threatening expressions and gestures, he insults us. Then, more gently, as to a large animal that needs to be reassured, he speaks to the truck in a murmur, before turning back to us once again to sputter his disapproval—"Bunch of losers!"

I sense confusedly that however crazy or drunk he might be, the man is probably right, and that there was something indecent in our gregarious eagerness to gather around the truck . . . Then I'm reminded of a certain cargo ship run aground just off the wharf at Cotonou, and how gigantic its hull looked when entirely out of the water. There too the sight had attracted gapers. Though, in this case, they avoided gathering in large numbers, spontaneously staggering their visits and never amounting to more than four or five at any one time, silent, solemn, each obviously steeped in the twin feeling of bearing witness to both greatness and death.

JUDITH QUEEN OF HEARTS

I've hardly finished evoking London, the Warren Street Station escalator, and my encounter there with Allori's *Judith*, before another scene comes back to me. In France, in Colomars, a small town in the backcountry of Nice. In a few hours' time, the voice of Dean Martin, one of Lulu's most favorite singers, will be resonating in the house as it does every day—unless it's Sam's voice we hear instead, tormented by some unsatisfied appetite. But, for the moment, a gratified Sam is sleeping soundly, Lulu and her partner are probably doing the same—at least, there's no crooner to be heard—and taking advantage of this lull, I pick up the work I left off last night. I have started writing my novel *Jojo*. The first chapter is finished, or nearly . . .

The years pass and I open to page fourteen of my personal copy to make sure I'm not having a false memory, one fabricated after the fact by my imagination.

> With every deal, we were sure to turn up the sword of the old tête-bêche king Charlemagne, with his surly looks, his white beard, his baldric worn on the diagonal and with little hearts in all four corners. If not him, then Judith, the bareheaded queen in her blue veil, whose pearl necklace and clasped flower look like the work of some prank artist who had transformed the lovely murderess into a gypsy fortune-teller cruising the corridors of the Paris metro.

No, there's no mistake, it was already my dear Jewess ("Judith" means "Jewess"), and along with her, the metro, already there—and already a queen's story . . . !

Naturally, how could I not be jubilant?

GÉRARD GAVARRY was born in Paris in 1946 and has also lived in New Caledonia, Niger, Guinea, Benin, and London. He studied literature at the Sorbonne and taught French literature first in Gabon and then in Paris. He is the author of nine books.

JANE KUNTZ has translated *Everyday Life* and *The Power of Flies* by Lydie Salvayre, *Hotel Crystal* by Olivier Rolin, *Pigeon Post* by Dumitru Tsepeneag, and *Hoppla! 1 2 3* by Gérard Gavarry, all of which are available from Dalkey Archive Press.

PETROS ABATZOGLOU, *What Does Mrs. Freeman Want?*

MICHAL AJVAZ, *The Golden Age.*
The Other City.

PIERRE ALBERT-BIROT, *Grabinoulor.*

YUZ ALESHKOVSKY, *Kangaroo.*

FELIPE ALFAU, *Chromos.*
Locos.

IVAN ÂNGELO, *The Celebration.*
The Tower of Glass.

DAVID ANTIN, *Talking.*

ANTÓNIO LOBO ANTUNES, *Knowledge of Hell.*

ALAIN ARIAS-MISSON, *Theatre of Incest.*

IFTIKHAR ARIF AND WAQAS KHWAJA, EDS., *Modern Poetry of Pakistan.*

JOHN ASHBERY AND JAMES SCHUYLER, *A Nest of Ninnies.*

GABRIELA AVIGUR-ROTEM, *Heatwave and Crazy Birds.*

HEIMRAD BÄCKER, *transcript.*

DJUNA BARNES, *Ladies Almanack.*
Ryder.

JOHN BARTH, *LETTERS.*
Sabbatical.

DONALD BARTHELME, *The King.*
Paradise.

SVETISLAV BASARA, *Chinese Letter.*

RENÉ BELLETTO, *Dying.*

MARK BINELLI, *Sacco and Vanzetti Must Die!*

ANDREI BITOV, *Pushkin House.*

ANDREJ BLATNIK, *You Do Understand.*

LOUIS PAUL BOON, *Chapel Road.*
My Little War.
Summer in Termuren.

ROGER BOYLAN, *Killoyle.*

IGNÁCIO DE LOYOLA BRANDÃO, *Anonymous Celebrity.*
The Good-Bye Angel.
Teeth under the Sun.
Zero.

BONNIE BREMSER, *Troia: Mexican Memoirs.*

CHRISTINE BROOKE-ROSE, *Amalgamemnon.*

BRIGID BROPHY, *In Transit.*

MEREDITH BROSNAN, *Mr. Dynamite.*

GERALD L. BRUNS, *Modern Poetry and the Idea of Language.*

EVGENY BUNIMOVICH AND J. KATES, EDS., *Contemporary Russian Poetry: An Anthology.*

GABRIELLE BURTON, *Heartbreak Hotel.*

MICHEL BUTOR, *Degrees.*
Mobile.
Portrait of the Artist as a Young Ape.

G. CABRERA INFANTE, *Infante's Inferno.*
Three Trapped Tigers.

JULIETA CAMPOS, *The Fear of Losing Eurydice.*

ANNE CARSON, *Eros the Bittersweet.*

ORLY CASTEL-BLOOM, *Dolly City.*

CAMILO JOSÉ CELA, *Christ versus Arizona.*
The Family of Pascual Duarte.
The Hive.

LOUIS-FERDINAND CÉLINE, *Castle to Castle.*
Conversations with Professor Y.
London Bridge.
Normance.
North.
Rigadoon.

HUGO CHARTERIS, *The Tide Is Right.*

JEROME CHARYN, *The Tar Baby.*

ERIC CHEVILLARD, *Demolishing Nisard.*

MARC CHOLODENKO, *Mordechai Schamz.*

JOSHUA COHEN, *Witz.*

EMILY HOLMES COLEMAN, *The Shutter of Snow.*

ROBERT COOVER, *A Night at the Movies.*

STANLEY CRAWFORD, *Log of the S.S. The Mrs Unguentine.*
Some Instructions to My Wife.

ROBERT CREELEY, *Collected Prose.*

RENÉ CREVEL, *Putting My Foot in It.*

RALPH CUSACK, *Cadenza.*

SUSAN DAITCH, *L.C.*
Storytown.

NICHOLAS DELBANCO, *The Count of Concord.*
Sherbrookes.

NIGEL DENNIS, *Cards of Identity.*

PETER DIMOCK, *A Short Rhetoric for Leaving the Family.*

ARIEL DORFMAN, *Konfidenz.*

COLEMAN DOWELL, *The Houses of Children.*
Island People.
Too Much Flesh and Jabez.

ARKADII DRAGOMOSHCHENKO, *Dust.*

RIKKI DUCORNET, *The Complete Butcher's Tales.*
The Fountains of Neptune.
The Jade Cabinet.
The One Marvelous Thing.
Phosphor in Dreamland.
The Stain.
The Word "Desire."

WILLIAM EASTLAKE, *The Bamboo Bed.*
Castle Keep.
Lyric of the Circle Heart.

JEAN ECHENOZ, *Chopin's Move.*

STANLEY ELKIN, *A Bad Man.*
Boswell: A Modern Comedy.
Criers and Kibitzers, Kibitzers and Criers.
The Dick Gibson Show.
The Franchiser.
George Mills.
The Living End.
The MacGuffin.
The Magic Kingdom.
Mrs. Ted Bliss.
The Rabbi of Lud.
Van Gogh's Room at Arles.

ANNIE ERNAUX, *Cleaned Out.*

LAUREN FAIRBANKS, *Muzzle Thyself.*
Sister Carrie.

LESLIE A. FIEDLER, *Love and Death in the American Novel.*

JUAN FILLOY, *Op Oloop.*

GUSTAVE FLAUBERT, *Bouvard and Pécuchet.*

KASS FLEISHER, *Talking out of School.*

FORD MADOX FORD, *The March of Literature.*

JON FOSSE, *Aliss at the Fire.*
Melancholy.

MAX FRISCH, *I'm Not Stiller.*
Man in the Holocene.

SELECTED DALKEY ARCHIVE PAPERBACKS

CARLOS FUENTES, *Christopher Unborn.*
Distant Relations.
Terra Nostra.
Where the Air Is Clear.
JANICE GALLOWAY, *Foreign Parts.*
The Trick Is to Keep Breathing.
WILLIAM H. GASS, *Cartesian Sonata and Other Novellas.*
Finding a Form.
A Temple of Texts.
The Tunnel.
Willie Masters' Lonesome Wife.
GÉRARD GAVARRY, *Hoppla! 1 2 3.*
Making a Novel.
ETIENNE GILSON,
The Arts of the Beautiful.
Forms and Substances in the Arts.
C. S. GISCOMBE, *Giscome Road.*
Here.
Prairie Style.
DOUGLAS GLOVER, *Bad News of the Heart.*
The Enamoured Knight.
WITOLD GOMBROWICZ,
A Kind of Testament.
KAREN ELIZABETH GORDON,
The Red Shoes.
GEORGI GOSPODINOV, *Natural Novel.*
JUAN GOYTISOLO, *Count Julian.*
Exiled from Almost Everywhere.
Juan the Landless.
Makbara.
Marks of Identity.
PATRICK GRAINVILLE, *The Cave of Heaven.*
HENRY GREEN, *Back.*
Blindness.
Concluding.
Doting.
Nothing.
JIŘÍ GRUŠA, *The Questionnaire.*
GABRIEL GUDDING,
Rhode Island Notebook.
MELA HARTWIG, *Am I a Redundant Human Being?*
JOHN HAWKES, *The Passion Artist.*
Whistlejacket.
ALEKSANDAR HEMON, ED.,
Best European Fiction.
AIDAN HIGGINS, *A Bestiary.*
Balcony of Europe.
Bornholm Night-Ferry.
Darkling Plain: Texts for the Air.
Flotsam and Jetsam.
Langrishe, Go Down.
Scenes from a Receding Past.
Windy Arbours.
KEIZO HINO, *Isle of Dreams.*
KAZUSHI HOSAKA, *Plainsong.*
ALDOUS HUXLEY, *Antic Hay.*
Crome Yellow.
Point Counter Point.
Those Barren Leaves.
Time Must Have a Stop.
NAOYUKI II, *The Shadow of a Blue Cat.*
MIKHAIL IOSSEL AND JEFF PARKER, EDS.,
Amerika: Russian Writers View the United States.
GERT JONKE, *The Distant Sound.*
Geometric Regional Novel.
Homage to Czerny.
The System of Vienna.

JACQUES JOUET, *Mountain R.*
Savage.
Upstaged.
CHARLES JULIET, *Conversations with Samuel Beckett and Bram van Velde.*
MIEKO KANAI, *The Word Book.*
YORAM KANIUK, *Life on Sandpaper.*
HUGH KENNER, *The Counterfeiters.*
Flaubert, Joyce and Beckett: The Stoic Comedians.
Joyce's Voices.
DANILO KIŠ, *Garden, Ashes.*
A Tomb for Boris Davidovich.
ANITA KONKKA, *A Fool's Paradise.*
GEORGE KONRÁD, *The City Builder.*
TADEUSZ KONWICKI, *A Minor Apocalypse.*
The Polish Complex.
MENIS KOUMANDAREAS, *Koula.*
ELAINE KRAF, *The Princess of 72nd Street.*
JIM KRUSOE, *Iceland.*
EWA KURYLUK, *Century 21.*
EMILIO LASCANO TEGUI, *On Elegance While Sleeping.*
ERIC LAURRENT, *Do Not Touch.*
HERVÉ LE TELLIER, *The Sextine Chapel.*
A Thousand Pearls (for a Thousand Pennies).
VIOLETTE LEDUC, *La Bâtarde.*
EDOUARD LEVÉ, *Suicide.*
SUZANNE JILL LEVINE, *The Subversive Scribe: Translating Latin American Fiction.*
DEBORAH LEVY, *Billy and Girl.*
Pillow Talk in Europe and Other Places.
JOSÉ LEZAMA LIMA, *Paradiso.*
ROSA LIKSOM, *Dark Paradise.*
OSMAN LINS, *Avalovara.*
The Queen of the Prisons of Greece.
ALF MAC LOCHLAINN, *The Corpus in the Library.*
Out of Focus.
RON LOEWINSOHN, *Magnetic Field(s).*
MINA LOY, *Stories and Essays of Mina Loy.*
BRIAN LYNCH, *The Winner of Sorrow.*
D. KEITH MANO, *Take Five.*
MICHELINE AHARONIAN MARCOM,
The Mirror in the Well.
BEN MARCUS,
The Age of Wire and String.
WALLACE MARKFIELD,
Teitlebaum's Window.
To an Early Grave.
DAVID MARKSON, *Reader's Block.*
Springer's Progress.
Wittgenstein's Mistress.
CAROLE MASO, *AVA.*
LADISLAV MATEJKA AND KRYSTYNA POMORSKA, EDS.,
Readings in Russian Poetics: Formalist and Structuralist Views.
HARRY MATHEWS,
The Case of the Persevering Maltese: Collected Essays.
Cigarettes.
The Conversions.
The Human Country: New and Collected Stories.
The Journalist.

FOR A FULL LIST OF PUBLICATIONS, VISIT:
www.dalkeyarchive.com

My Life in CIA.
Singular Pleasures.
The Sinking of the Odradek
  Stadium.
Tlooth.
20 Lines a Day.
JOSEPH MCELROY,
  Night Soul and Other Stories.
THOMAS MCGONIGLE,
  Going to Patchogue.
ROBERT L. MCLAUGHLIN, ED., *Innovations:*
  An Anthology of
  Modern & Contemporary Fiction.
ABDELWAHAB MEDDEB, *Talismano.*
HERMAN MELVILLE, *The Confidence-Man.*
AMANDA MICHALOPOULOU, *I'd Like.*
STEVEN MILLHAUSER,
  The Barnum Museum.
  In the Penny Arcade.
RALPH J. MILLS, JR.,
  Essays on Poetry.
MOMUS, *The Book of Jokes.*
CHRISTINE MONTALBETTI, *Western.*
OLIVE MOORE, *Spleen.*
NICHOLAS MOSLEY, *Accident.*
  Assassins.
  Catastrophe Practice.
  Children of Darkness and Light.
  Experience and Religion.
  God's Hazard.
  The Hesperides Tree.
  Hopeful Monsters.
  Imago Bird.
  Impossible Object.
  Inventing God.
  Judith.
  Look at the Dark.
  Natalie Natalia.
  Paradoxes of Peace.
  Serpent.
  Time at War.
  The Uses of Slime Mould:
    Essays of Four Decades.
WARREN MOTTE,
  Fables of the Novel: French Fiction
    since 1990.
  Fiction Now: The French Novel in
    the 21st Century.
  Oulipo: A Primer of Potential
    Literature.
YVES NAVARRE, *Our Share of Time.*
  Sweet Tooth.
DOROTHY NELSON, *In Night's City.*
  Tar and Feathers.
ESHKOL NEVO, *Homesick.*
WILFRIDO D. NOLLEDO, *But for the Lovers.*
FLANN O'BRIEN,
  At Swim-Two-Birds.
  At War.
  The Best of Myles.
  The Dalkey Archive.
  Further Cuttings.
  The Hard Life.
  The Poor Mouth.
  The Third Policeman.
CLAUDE OLLIER, *The Mise-en-Scène.*
  Wert and the Life Without End.
PATRIK OUŘEDNÍK, *Europeana.*
  The Opportune Moment, 1855.
BORIS PAHOR, *Necropolis.*

FERNANDO DEL PASO,
  News from the Empire.
  Palinuro of Mexico.
ROBERT PINGET, *The Inquisitory.*
  Mahu or The Material.
  Trio.
MANUEL PUIG,
  Betrayed by Rita Hayworth.
  The Buenos Aires Affair.
  Heartbreak Tango.
RAYMOND QUENEAU, *The Last Days.*
  Odile.
  Pierrot Mon Ami.
  Saint Glinglin.
ANN QUIN, *Berg.*
  Passages.
  Three.
  Tripticks.
ISHMAEL REED,
  The Free-Lance Pallbearers.
  The Last Days of Louisiana Red.
  Ishmael Reed: The Plays.
  Juice!
  Reckless Eyeballing.
  The Terrible Threes.
  The Terrible Twos.
  Yellow Back Radio Broke-Down.
JOÃO UBALDO RIBEIRO, *House of the*
    Fortunate Buddhas.
JEAN RICARDOU, *Place Names.*
RAINER MARIA RILKE, *The Notebooks of*
    Malte Laurids Brigge.
JULIÁN RÍOS, *The House of Ulysses.*
  Larva: A Midsummer Night's Babel.
  Poundemonium.
  Procession of Shadows.
AUGUSTO ROA BASTOS, *I the Supreme.*
DANIËL ROBBERECHTS,
  Arriving in Avignon.
JEAN ROLIN, *The Explosion of the*
    Radiator Hose.
OLIVIER ROLIN, *Hotel Crystal.*
ALIX CLEO ROUBAUD, *Alix's Journal.*
JACQUES ROUBAUD, *The Form of a*
    City Changes Faster, Alas, Than
    the Human Heart.
  The Great Fire of London.
  Hortense in Exile.
  Hortense Is Abducted.
  The Loop.
  The Plurality of Worlds of Lewis.
  The Princess Hoppy.
  Some Thing Black.
LEON S. ROUDIEZ, *French Fiction Revisited.*
RAYMOND ROUSSEL, *Impressions of Africa.*
VEDRANA RUDAN, *Night.*
STIG SÆTERBAKKEN, *Siamese.*
LYDIE SALVAYRE, *The Company of Ghosts.*
  Everyday Life.
  The Lecture.
  Portrait of the Writer as a
    Domesticated Animal.
  The Power of Flies.
LUIS RAFAEL SÁNCHEZ,
  Macho Camacho's Beat.
SEVERO SARDUY, *Cobra & Maitreya.*
NATHALIE SARRAUTE,
  Do You Hear Them?
  Martereau.
  The Planetarium.

SELECTED DALKEY ARCHIVE PAPERBACKS

ARNO SCHMIDT, *Collected Novellas.*
Collected Stories.
Nobodaddy's Children.
Two Novels.
ASAF SCHURR, *Motti.*
CHRISTINE SCHUTT, *Nightwork.*
GAIL SCOTT, *My Paris.*
DAMION SEARLS, *What We Were Doing
and Where We Were Going.*
JUNE AKERS SEESE,
Is This What Other Women Feel Too?
What Waiting Really Means.
BERNARD SHARE, *Inish.*
Transit.
AURELIE SHEEHAN,
Jack Kerouac Is Pregnant.
VIKTOR SHKLOVSKY, *Bowstring.*
Knight's Move.
*A Sentimental Journey:
Memoirs 1917–1922.*
Energy of Delusion: A Book on Plot.
Literature and Cinematography.
Theory of Prose.
Third Factory.
Zoo, or Letters Not about Love.
CLAUDE SIMON, *The Invitation.*
PIERRE SINIAC, *The Collaborators.*
JOSEF ŠKVORECKÝ, *The Engineer of
Human Souls.*
GILBERT SORRENTINO,
Aberration of Starlight.
Blue Pastoral.
Crystal Vision.
*Imaginative Qualities of Actual
Things.*
Mulligan Stew.
Pack of Lies.
Red the Fiend.
The Sky Changes.
Something Said.
Splendide-Hôtel.
Steelwork.
Under the Shadow.
W. M. SPACKMAN,
The Complete Fiction.
ANDRZEJ STASIUK, *Fado.*
GERTRUDE STEIN,
Lucy Church Amiably.
The Making of Americans.
A Novel of Thank You.
LARS SVENDSEN, *A Philosophy of Evil.*
PIOTR SZEWC, *Annihilation.*
GONÇALO M. TAVARES, *Jerusalem.*
*Learning to Pray in the Age of
Technology.*
LUCIAN DAN TEODOROVICI,
Our Circus Presents . . .
STEFAN THEMERSON, *Hobson's Island.*
The Mystery of the Sardine.
Tom Harris.
JOHN TOOMEY, *Sleepwalker.*
JEAN-PHILIPPE TOUSSAINT,
The Bathroom.
Camera.
Monsieur.
Running Away.
Self-Portrait Abroad.
Television.
DUMITRU TSEPENEAG,
Hotel Europa.

The Necessary Marriage.
Pigeon Post.
Vain Art of the Fugue.
ESTHER TUSQUETS, *Stranded.*
DUBRAVKA UGRESIC,
Lend Me Your Character.
Thank You for Not Reading.
MATI UNT, *Brecht at Night.*
Diary of a Blood Donor.
Things in the Night.
ÁLVARO URIBE AND OLIVIA SEARS, EDS.,
*Best of Contemporary Mexican
Fiction.*
ELOY URROZ, *Friction.*
The Obstacles.
LUISA VALENZUELA, *Dark Desires and
the Others.*
He Who Searches.
MARJA-LIISA VARTIO,
The Parson's Widow.
PAUL VERHAEGHEN, *Omega Minor.*
BORIS VIAN, *Heartsnatcher.*
LLORENÇ VILLALONGA, *The Dolls' Room.*
ORNELA VORPSI, *The Country Where No
One Ever Dies.*
AUSTRYN WAINHOUSE, *Hedyphagetica.*
PAUL WEST,
Words for a Deaf Daughter & Gala.
CURTIS WHITE,
America's Magic Mountain.
The Idea of Home.
Memories of My Father Watching TV.
*Monstrous Possibility: An Invitation
to Literary Politics.*
Requiem.
DIANE WILLIAMS, *Excitability:
Selected Stories.*
Romancer Erector.
DOUGLAS WOOLF, *Wall to Wall.*
Ya! & John-Juan.
JAY WRIGHT, *Polynomials and Pollen.*
*The Presentable Art of Reading
Absence.*
PHILIP WYLIE, *Generation of Vipers.*
MARGUERITE YOUNG, *Angel in the Forest.*
Miss MacIntosh, My Darling.
REYOUNG, *Unbabbling.*
VLADO ŽABOT, *The Succubus.*
ZORAN ŽIVKOVIĆ, *Hidden Camera.*
LOUIS ZUKOFSKY, *Collected Fiction.*
SCOTT ZWIREN, *God Head.*

FOR A FULL LIST OF PUBLICATIONS, VISIT:
www.dalkeyarchive.com